It is what it is

A positive guide to facing up to life changing events – events that would require great inner strength, courage and positivity to overcome. Qualities that were needed to tackle the devastating life-changing events that were to shatter a calm, serene life including the ultimate life-changing event – GRIEF. This book portrays an honest account of the true feelings of disbelief, despair and grief, not often spoken about.

Copyright © 2022 by Julie Morehen. All rights reserved.

This book or any portion thereof may not be reproduced or used in any manner whatsoever without the express written permission of the publisher except for the use of brief quotations in a book review.

Strenuous attempts have been made to credit all copyrighted materials used in this book. All such materials and trademarks, which are referenced in this book, are the full property of their respective copyright owners. Every effort has been made to obtain copyright permission for material quoted in this book. Any omissions will be rectified in future editions.

Cover image and book design by: Ivan Sage

Printed in the United Kingdom
First Printing, 2022

ISBN: 978-1-7397327-0-7 (Paperback)
ISBN: 978-1-7397327-1-4 (eBook)

Wild Flowers Publishing
Colchester, Essex

Juliemorehen205@gmail.com

-oOo-

*Dedicated to the memory of
Cameron 'Cas' Morehen
17.4.1955 – 20.10.2018*

-oOo-

INTRODUCTION

By Ivan Sage

IF YOU have recently experienced a major setback in your life or a bereavement the chances are you are feeling at your lowest ebb right now but, unlike many books on such subjects, this one has a message running through it – a message of POSITIVITY.

Adopting a positive attitude can prove to be a vital ingredient to help you rebuild your life. Julie Morehen is a fine example of this for, as you will soon read, following the death of her husband Cas, she was not only at the depths of despair – her loss prompted her to behave in a way that was totally out of character.

Julie began to experience bizarre and extreme emotions following her bereavement. In fact, that might even be described as an understatement – these were *really* extreme thoughts that, at times, featured malicious and unpleasant attitudes towards other people.

Admittedly, such emotions are rarely admitted to – some people, although feeling this way, do their utmost to mask their malevolent thoughts from others but, in some cases, this just isn't possible.

Sometimes these thoughts prove just too powerful for a person to hold back and this can, quite understandably, lead other people to be greatly offended by the comments or actions of a bereaved person who expresses such feelings at any given time.

Julie's reactions to the death of her husband Cas may have been difficult for some of her friends and family to understand or accept. By turning away sympathetic messages and the support of well-intentioned acquaintances she ran the risk of alienating herself from the very people who cared about her, this at a time when the vast majority of people in Julie's situation would have most needed support.

Hopefully, after reading this account of Julie's journey following Cas's untimely death, readers will begin to understand how and why Julie's reactions to her loss were beyond her control and did not accurately reflect the kind of person she really is.

Grief, for sure, is such a deeply intense and deeply personal emotion. We all have to find our own ways of dealing with the loss of a loved one as there is no easy one-fits-all solution to such a traumatic and life-changing experience.

Yet grief is a vital part of the healing experience. Bottling up feelings of utter wretchedness benefit no-one. Allowing grief to be expressed is akin to the releasing of steam from a pressure cooker.

That said, your grief cannot be allowed to rule the rest of your life. Like it or not, life does go on and this requires negative emotions to be challenged in such a way to ensure that you can still make your life more bearable, even enjoyable, again at some point in the future.

Julie believes that one can draw on life experiences – good and bad. Can you remember how you reacted at those times? Did you feel that you were never going to recover, become stronger, but you did? You can dig deep, use your past and present strengths and confidence to enable you to recover from this devastating experience.

Plan A may have vanished but, with the right attitude, you may find a Plan B that, although much different to what you may have envisaged, may eventually turn out to be a reasonable substitute.

I have to imagine that, by reading this, you will have recently experienced a loss of this kind and that you are struggling to come to terms with the tsunami of emotions that threaten to overwhelm any one of us at some time or another.

While some may feel their world has ended after the death of someone who has been much loved, others may feel the time has come to deal with their situation in a more pragmatic manner.

Some people may have the support of family and friends, others not. Some may have the financial means to deal with the situation they have been left in, while others may be wondering how on earth they will cope both financially and/or on a practical level.

And, of course, the manner of a loved one's death will, inevitably, play a huge part in the way those left behind are able to cope with their situation.

It may be stating the obvious, but a sudden, unexpected death gives the bereaved no time at all to prepare while the death of someone following a long terminal illness, while also devastating, at least gives the bereaved the opportunity to mentally prepare for the inevitable.

Furthermore, the age of the deceased, whether he or she may have been a small child or an elderly person, will evoke widely differing emotions amongst those left behind.

So, before we go too far, let's just make a couple of things clear . . .

Firstly, however you are feeling right now . . . it's okay. There is no rule book on how you should be feeling at a time of loss.

You are an individual.

Your emotions are your own way of coping with your situation. Perhaps you will be fortunate enough to be offered the help and support of family and friends. On the other hand, if such support is not available, if you feel totally alone, try to reach out for advice and practical help from one of the organisations set up specifically to assist the bereaved. You will find an index of some of these helpful services at the end of this book.

You do not have to face this alone.

Maybe, though, you are an independent or more private person who prefers to deal with your situation completely on your own. That's okay too. Whatever works for you is the right way forward.

This is Julie's personal account of how she dealt with the death of her husband Cas in *her* own way and how, despite her crippling emotions at the time, she has since slowly but surely begun to rebuild her life. She recalls other past life-changing events and the lessons learnt, how these shaped the person she has become – a person that could dig really deep and find the resources necessary to survive the most devastating event of all.

Unlike many readers, we have to acknowledge that Julie was left financially secure following Cas's death and this has enabled her to follow a path that she rightly accepts most readers may not be in a position to follow.

However, it was another of Cas's legacies that Julie hopes she can pass on to readers, rich or poor, that she hopes may enable them to find a light at the end of the long, dark tunnel currently before them . . .

* * *

Julie was absolutely devastated when her beloved husband Cameron (Cas) died suddenly and unexpectedly in October 2018. In an instant all the couple's dreams and plans for the future had been wiped out and 58-year-old Julie was left to face a future without the man with whom she had shared her life and love over the past 33 years.

A year later, however, Julie was slowly beginning to rebuild her life and looking forward to a brighter future, thanks to Cas's priceless legacy – A Positive Mental Attitude.

This account describes how the most traumatic event by far in Julie's life has been tackled head-on despite the demons in her mind that had so often threatened to push her into the abyss.

Julie's thoughts and emotions in the months following Cas's death were not as she might have foreseen. Besides the feelings of heartbreak that anyone would have expected her to experience, Julie found herself overwhelmed by many dark and embittered thoughts which, for her, were totally out of character.

I would be lying if I was to say I felt comfortable about some of Julie's comments when we began writing this book. We had never met before so I had very little idea of the type of person I would be working with and, at first, I have to admit, I found some of her perspectives on life since bereavement to be harsh to say the very least.

Now, having completed this project, I can more appreciate why she felt the way she did and how the hardened demeanour she adopted after Cas's death had helped her to come through such a traumatic experience.

It takes a brave person to describe so openly these malevolent emotions as Julie does in this book – particularly when some of those misguided sentiments were even directed towards much-loved family members and friends – people who she now acknowledges only had her best interests at heart.

Her honestly-disclosed revelations have made me wonder how many other people who have suffered the loss of a loved one could empathise with her – how many people have actually shared such pernicious thoughts but have not had the courage to admit to them?

But Julie is not an unpleasant individual – these feelings did not reflect who she really is – a kind, caring and generous person. This was a period of time that Julie had to come face-to-face with a maelstrom of emotions – a rage within – that she had very little control over at the time.

I believe Julie's sometimes harsh attitude towards others was a protective shield to her otherwise delicate state of mind and I really hope that when you first read of some of the deeply unpleasant thoughts that pervaded her mind throughout her darker days that you will not judge her too harshly for, as this story unfolds, it will become clearer that those sometimes malicious thoughts certainly do not reflect Julie's character.

The fact that she has decided to openly acknowledge a wide range of feelings such as anger, jealousy and resentfulness says a lot about her as a person – a person who now wants to help other bereaved individuals to come to terms with their loss.

Julie wants you to understand that it is not abnormal to feel anger, bitterness, resentment – even hatred. Very few will admit to having those feelings but some of you reading this will, in fact, recognise themselves.

Following Cas's death Julie read at least half a dozen books based on coping with grief but failed to find one that truly connected with her state of mind at the time. Then she recalled Cas's laid-back 'whatever will be' look on life and decided she had to adopt a similar attitude if she was to make it through the darkest period of her life – and that was the inspiration for this story.

She remembered seeing many books and quotes relating to the American author Dale Carnegie. Julie informed me that Cas was passionate about this author's work and that he had applied the knowledge gained from Carnegie to all aspects of his life. Some of the quotes irritated Julie as they were often spoken when Cas could not win an argument – for example – 'It is what it is'.

Julie would later find that these quotations inspired her to recover in a way that was not just surviving but living! Such quotations would later be passed onto other bereaved friends as Julie navigated her way through her long, arduous journey.

Of course there will be sadness within some of the passages that follow – it would not be possible to write about this subject without it. Hopefully, though, readers will appreciate what Julie is trying to communicate – that a Positive Mental Attitude can work wonders in forcing back the heavy, dark veil of grief – a grief that she can only describe as a grey, hovering cloud that follows you around. Suddenly, and without warning, it engulfs your whole body, leaving you helpless, scared and irrational.

Julie is now beginning to rebuild her life. That is not to say that she does not still mourn her husband, because she certainly does – it just means she believes that, by taking stock of a situation, and taking positive steps forward, the crippling grief so commonly experienced can be alleviated to such a degree that it is eventually possible to face the future in a much better and more positive frame of mind.

This is an account of how, despite her loss, Julie has emerged from a heart-breaking situation to a place in her life that, having adopted Cas's legacy of positivity, she can now put those dark thoughts to one side. She can now begin to live her life and look forward to a brighter future.

She has, at last, rediscovered her own identity; 'her old self'. She has largely – though not completely – banished those negative thoughts; gained confidence; made plans for her future; set and achieved goals; and found an inner strength and confidence that she knew was there but had doubted that she could ever regain.

Cas and Julie were very fortunate to have shared a deep love for each other – and a *very* comfortable lifestyle. As already mentioned, this has meant that Julie has had opportunities to tackle her grief in many ways that other, less fortunate people may not have had.

This is a fact that Julie has not overlooked. Not many bereaved individuals find themselves without the worry of bills and mortgages to pay but, at the end of the day, no amount of money can compensate for the emotional rollercoaster that follows the death of a loved one.

Certainly those who may believe that someone who is financially secure does not feel an equally devastating form of grief compared to someone without such a safety net are in the minority.

This was clearly demonstrated following an editorial published in *The Guardian* in 2019 which caused outrage when it was suggested that former Prime Minister David Cameron's grief at losing his six-year-old disabled son Ivan was a form of *'privileged pain'*.

Such was the outpouring of condemnation against *The Guardian's* article it bowed to public pressure by publishing an apology and deleted the article from its website.

It must be acknowledged that there is no magic wand or overnight cure for grief, and that Julie's approach to a dreadful, life-changing event would not work for everyone. And, it has to be admitted, that Julie's journey is not yet at its end – it is still work in progress.

This story, in its way, has been another aspect of Julie's healing process – a cathartic experience if you like – but her primary reason for getting her thoughts and experiences laid out in print is that she hopes others will be able to benefit from her personal journey through life challenges, including bereavement.

I hope that readers can take inspiration from her story and that, at some point, they will be able find it within themselves to face their own future in a much more positive frame of mind.

Finally, I'd like to end with a quote by American Lebanese-Jordanian businessman and motivational speaker Nido Quebein which, I hope, may inspire you to face the future:

'Your present circumstances don't determine
where you can go;
they merely determine where you start.'

FOREWORD

THIS is a book I wish I had never felt the need to write.

The death of my husband Cas in October 2018 dramatically turned my hitherto happy life upside down and, suddenly, I had to face an uncertain future and, with it, the fears, grief, feelings of loss and everything else that inevitably followed my unplanned, unwanted new situation.

So why put all those experiences and feelings down on paper? Well, first of all, following Cas's untimely death I began to write a journal in which my most private thoughts were recorded.

The journal started on day one with the words 'devastation, hell, hysteria, screaming, desperation and questions – so many questions'. Day two recorded all of those feelings with the added words 'shaking and disbelief'.

The following days and weeks recorded my reactions to the many messages, flowers and cards and the dramatic decline in my health, both physically and mentally. Further into the journal I recorded the practical tasks achieved.

Very, very soon, I expressed feelings of a rage and hatred of the world and of those around me. Those feelings were to stay with me for a very long time. I found that a huge burden to bear.

After several months I decided that the notes from my journal should go down in a more readable format for three main reasons:
1. To remind myself of how bad I was feeling at that time. So that I could revisit those thoughts and monitor my very gradual improvement, both mentally and physically
2. That my feelings and experiences could be used to help others who have suddenly been thrust into a similar situation.
3. That the huge burden of carrying those feelings would somehow be alleviated.

I wanted to write this account as it was an approach that was unique to me. Grief is a personal journey and the early choices made on the journey will determine your recovery. Very early, I chose to recover.

To reflect those deeply personal feelings throughout this book, I will quote some of the exact words/sentences that are written in my journal. These will appear randomly throughout the book.

I hope that this will give you an insight into the fragility of my mind. As I read through it for this very purpose, I cannot believe that I am the same person but, strangely, the words do not upset me but bring me great sadness that I could have even felt, yet alone expressed, such vindictive thoughts.

The road that I am on may differ to that of many other widows. I was fortunate to have had a positive husband, positive boys and, eventually, a positive approach to bereavement which, I believe, has helped me enormously – and that's a message I really hope will come across to readers.

As a newly-bereaved widow I was desperate for information and I sought out several books on the subject, some of which were helpful, others not so. I guess the benefits gained from books depend largely upon the type of person you are and your personal circumstances.

Some books did not detail some of the more bizarre things you might think or do when you are grieving and, soon, you will read that my own reactions to grief may not necessarily be the norm – or were they?

I began to wonder if my more extreme reactions were unique to me or did other people sometimes feel the same way but, perhaps, they would not express them so openly as I had?

I know for sure that I behaved most erratically and most books on bereavement didn't touch on that aspect. I began to feel as if my feelings and actions were not normal. I began to question my sanity. And then I came across one book which did touch on this aspect and, suddenly, I realised I wasn't alone. Maybe I wasn't going mad after all!

Having joined various forums and groups since Cas's death, and having spoken to other bereaved people in depth, I now realise my sometimes malevolent thoughts were not exclusive to me.
Some of the crazy ideas that popped into my head after my loss could have had a terrible impact on my life had I followed them through. Making major decisions at such a time is, on reflection, not a good idea. It is, instead, a time to take stock of your situation and to calmly consider your life's path moving forward. But being calm is something that is not an instant emotion.
Positivity has played a major role in my personal journey through life's challenges. I believe that, as a family, we have tackled the grieving process head on and even embraced it. We have all worked so hard to never let it completely engulf us.
Admittedly, that has not always been easy – far from it – but I am convinced that a positive outlook has not only benefited me, but also my family on this sudden, unplanned and unwanted journey.

–o0o–

'You're allowed to scream, you're allowed to cry, but do not give up'
Unknown

–o0o–

In a moment you will read of my journey through life's challenges – challenges that were overcome to lead me to having a happy and contented life. A chapter in my life where there was contentment, achievement, love and stability– a life that was shattered the moment I lost Cas. For some time I was convinced that future happiness would be beyond my reach as I desperately sought for assurances that I would 'be alright'.
Ironically, it is because of Cas that I now believe that I will be. I hope my experiences and advice will be of some help to those of you who have lost a loved one. However you are

feeling right now I want to reassure you that there can still be a reasonable future ahead of you.
I hope after reading this you will find yourself in a more positive state of mind and that you will be able, not to *move on* – I hate that term – but to *move forward*.
One chapter of your life has ended. Let's try now, without brushing aside the good times and love we once shared and treasured, to move forward with our lives in a positive way and to try our best to make new memories.

–o0o–

'A life-changing experience does not have to mean a life-ending one'
Sent to me by my son Stephen every day for weeks.

–o0o–

There are so many experiences that can have a devastating affect on people's lives. For that reason I am including two other aspects of my own life that had a traumatic affect on me at the time but these experiences have, I believe, given me the strength, positivity and determination to get through the even tougher times I encountered following Cas's death.

I'd had a very happy childhood. I was part of an Army family and had lived in several places, including Cyprus and Aden. The family eventually settled down in the coastal resort of Jaywick, adjacent to Clacton-on-Sea in Essex.
Although it may be hard to believe by those that know me, I was a very quiet, shy girl. I had good friends and I enjoyed school life. I was one of four children living with our parents David and Marian and my dear nan Hilda.
My father ran an ice cream van and the family also ran burger vans at race circuits. I was the envy of all my friends! Then Dad found work in the nearby town of Harwich as a taxi driver and, from that point on, none of us saw much of him. It would

be a few years later that the reason for his absence would be revealed.

First love and abuse

Paul (not his real name) was my first boyfriend. We met when I was just 16 years old. Despite my family's reservations about him, I ignored their advice to end the relationship.

Paul was a heavy drinker, something my dad was not happy with but I was in love, or so I thought! I guess the 16-year-old me did not take too kindly to my family finding fault in my first ever boyfriend. Their opinions though were justified. I can see that now. To have a boyfriend who would constantly bring you harm was not right.

I started my nursing training at 18, living in the nurses' home at Essex County Hospital in Colchester. I never attended doctors' parties or went out with friends. I was denied the chance to truly embrace the life of a trainee nurse living away from home for the first time.

Instead, at every opportunity, I drove back to Clacton to stay in the bedsit with Paul – after all, I was in love and very much being controlled – a control that would play on my kind nature and last for six years – a control that would make me feel guilty at every opportunity if I didn't see him.

There were occasions that I feared for my safety after yet another onslaught of verbal rage and physical threats and often actions. To name but a few, I had petrol poured over me with the threat to 'light the match', scarves tied around my neck and a broken cheekbone caused by kicking my face whilst I was on the ground.

But, in my mind, these incidents were deserved, it was my fault as I must have provoked him! – another aspect of self-guilt instilled in you by the abuser as they take control of everything, including your mind.

My life involved abuse in many forms and a regular intake of magic mushrooms (LSD) and cannabis, all whilst training to be a nurse! I am not proud of this confession and can hardly believe that I ever qualified.

When I was 19 years old Paul was sent to a young offenders' unit for two years – he had set fire to his mother's house while she was in it. This gave me a much-needed release from the traumas of everyday life.

In my 21st year, the relationship with Paul picked up from where it had left off. I felt guilty that he had no-one to come home to, other than me. Of course, he told me he had changed but, of course he hadn't! However I had become stronger in every aspect and was biding my time until I would tell Paul that we were over.

My decision to be with Paul for those six years, despite their concerns, had caused upset with my family that took several years to heal. Tough times for us all, for sure.

However, the strengths, determination and self-worth qualities that I had found in our time apart would come into play a few years later and again at the time of my loss.

I attempted to end my relationship with Paul several times. Finally, I was brave enough to leave a note declaring that 'we're over' and sneak out of the bedsit. The day, a Thursday, is so engrained on my mind because, as I walked down the path, he threw a glass milk bottle at my head – it just missed! He shouted: 'I'll hunt you down, if I can't have you, no-one will!'

For the next year, I endured threats and constant stalking of my daily activities – only ending when I moved out of the area.

Dad becomes Mandy

I had never known a lot about my dad's past and I wanted to gain a better understanding of why he made such a life-changing decision so, recently, I decided to 'interview' Mum to find out as much as possible.

This is her account:

The family name McElroy was the name we all grew up with. However, this name was chosen after Dad's mum had met a Scottish sailor and she liked his surname – McElroy. Dad had been told that his father's name was Dunn and his dad had died. Unfortunately, no-one could really confirm this.
Nannie McElroy was a well-known East London 'lady of the night' (a prostitute). Dad had told mum that there were frequent visits from men both day and night. It wasn't unusual for Dad and his brother Ted to return from school to find strangers in their home.
Both boys had witnessed their mum being beaten by drunken men and, sometimes, the boys would endure some physical abuse. Both Dad and Ted became tea-total. I never saw Dad drink alcohol.
Dad went into the army at a young age. He married Mum when she was 19 years old. She bought her own engagement ring! Mum recalls that Nannie McElroy made several attempts to persuade Mum not to marry my dad. His mum was aware at this time that Dad had become fixated with women's clothes and lifestyles.
We finally moved to Cyprus when I was six months old. Aden followed then, without notice, Dad was discharged from the army – the reason for this was never disclosed.
I remember when our family of five moved to Colchester and the catering empire was set up. The business was called DAMA Catering – DA for David, MA for Marian. A few ice cream and burger vans were purchased with Rossi ice cream

being sold. As teenagers, my friends and I would work on these vans – we had a great time. By the time my sister Jeanette came along, we were living in Jaywick. My mum still lives in the same house – she has been there for the past 50 years.

Dad started taxi driving in Harwich. Most of the family had not seen him for such a long time. Mum had been in contact by phone but he was no longer coming home. To us children it was as if he'd just disappeared. Then, one day, my mother met an acquaintance who asked her how Dad's operation had gone. Mum was confused. 'What operation? What are you talking about?'

It was at this point Mum was informed that, all the while Dad had been away from home, he had been cross-dressing and taking hormone treatment for his transition into becoming a woman! Mum was devastated by this revelation as she'd had absolutely no idea.

My Dad completed the transition from male to female (gender realignment) at the age of 46, becoming known around the town of Harwich as Mandy, the name of my favourite doll. It would be many, many years before I saw him again.

My brother Martin was, at this time, serving in the Army, my sister Jeanette was living in Germany, and my other brother Stephen, living in Buckinghamshire. At first it was decided not to tell Jeanette as she was in Germany and, for now, she didn't need to know.

Stephen, when he heard about Dad's secret life, was horrified – so much so that he changed his name by deed poll as he no longer wished to be associated with the family name. Martin, on the other hand, did not react so drastically but never saw Dad again.

Mum did keep in touch with him from time to time. It was on my 40th birthday, when I was married with two children, that I decided to meet Dad. Approximately 20 years had passed since we had seen each other. I travelled to Harwich with Mum to meet him.

I must give huge credit to my mum with whom, until he died, was regularly in touch with Dad. Mum remarried and her and Dennis would sometimes have lunch with Dad and I – a seemingly bizarre situation to others but a reasonable one to the four of us.

I would continue to see Dad as often as possible but it would take me years to tell my boys about him. I was worried how they would react, if it would embarrass them. My worries were not confirmed as they were brilliant in their support for me and, indeed, their granddad. Dad insisted that they call him Dave, not Mandy.

My three boys met him in their late teens, early twenties, as did their partners, and then Jack, his great grandson – who called him Nannie! He shared a few Christmas days with us all.

The family days spent with Dad were filled with his stories and his never-ending banter. He was a vibrant character and never stopped chatting. He had absorbed a wealth of knowledge over his years and knew so much about the war years – any history events. He had a very inquisitive mind. I often wonder if his thirst for knowledge and new possibilities led him to his journey of the transition?

Dad and I would go out to lunch. People would stare at his appearance. He had become female but didn't really look female. He would dress in trousers, big coats – as if he was trying to hide his obvious bust – which was bigger than mine! His voice was deep, his hands were big and, on occasions, I would find him still smoking his pipe! We would laugh so much about that.

The calm before the storm.

My family grew, I babysat more, my mum required more support and I worked more hours in the nursing home. I didn't see Dad as often as maybe I should have done. He started becoming obsessive about his health, demanding and verbally aggressive to others. He was seeking attention from everyone; NHS, councillors, shop keepers, neighbours and me.

Dad would regularly phone 999, stating that he needed urgent help. Many times he would be admitted to hospital and would be happily residing in a female ward whilst wearing a pink nightie. He loved the banter with the other ladies, talking about cooking etc. On visiting I would greet him with a hug and a 'hello Dad.' This created much confusion.

I would be called many times by staff who knew me well – I worked at the hospital – and they would tell me 'we have your mum here again.' I would reply, 'which one?'

Dad hated being discharged and would often say that he felt suicidal so that he would have to stay in and be assessed. This was clearly the early signs that his mind was fragile.

Eventually, I could see that Dad required more support. He had started to neglect his personal care and his mind was becoming paranoid and frantic. I managed to secure a place in a residential home in Clacton. Dad was okay about this, helping me to pack his things.

The journey by car from Harwich to Clacton though was fraught with questions, excessive talking and paranoia. At one point Dad grabbed the steering wheel and vowed to kill us both by crashing the car. I'll never forget the screaming and wailing from Dad as he experienced a psychotic episode. The mental health crisis team, paramedics and police were all alerted. I was told to try and get Dad to a place of safety that I knew, and that they would meet me there.

Dad and I arrived at Mum's house, the house that Dad had once lived in. Dad calmed down once inside and reverted to chatting, laughing – as if nothing had happened. It had been a surreal episode in my life.

Under the Mental Health Act, Dad was a danger to himself and, possibly, others. He was admitted to a secure mental health unit. His fragile mind had deteriorated to the point that he didn't understand what had happened in the past. He kept asking if he was male or female, why were some people calling him Mandy, Dave or Dad?

He died six weeks later, aged 85 years old. It was so, so sad that he should die in a confused, deranged way. He is buried in Harwich. His wooden cross reads David McElroy (Mandy).

It was a challenging time from the early discovery about Dad to the end but I'm glad I was faced with that challenge. It confirmed that I could show compassion and understanding during the most unusual circumstances.

The two challenging past events gave me a realisation of 'shit happens' to anyone and it can present itself in the most surprising of ways. These events have given me a reasonable level of resistance that has, no doubt, played it's part in my journey of recovery.

I've always known that few are untouched by trauma, life-changing events and tragedy. I thought I had been dealt my fair share – obviously not. But maybe these were presented to me by fate. Did fate play its part in preparing me for what was yet to come?

Ying and Yang

WHEN I first met Cas at his birthday party in his flat in Stepney Green, London in April 1983 there was an instant attraction between us. I would later move into his flat. It was only then that the stalking from Paul stopped as I was no longer in Clacton.

I had come along as the companion of one of Cas's invited friends and I was hugely looking forward to a crazy-sounding flan-throwing beach party where paper plates covered in shaving foam would be unceremoniously thrust into party-goers faces!

At the time I was 22 years old and Cas was 28. He was one of three children, being a twin to Christine and brother to his older sister Jen. His mum Peggy lived in Clacton. His dad died at the age of 46. Cas was only 12 at the time.

Cas was a decent guy. He had a good family background and he was kind and considerate. He had a car and a steady job as the manager of the Kensington High Street branch of McDonald's fast food restaurant. I was instantly smitten.

Meeting Cas at the party was the turning point in my life. We soon decided we wanted to be together. He proposed less than a year later by placing the ring inside a Christmas cracker!

I learned that Cas had originally lived in Clacton, not far from where I had been living with my family, although I had never met him before. He was a clever guy. He had been a pupil at Clacton County High School and had studied at Lancaster University where he gained a Bachelor of Arts in Economics and Marketing – a qualification that was to help him (and us) enormously in later life.

He was also a very good-looking guy – resembling 1970's pop heart-throb David Cassidy – hence his nickname Cas, his real name being Cameron. I now had my knight in shining armour, he had literally rescued me from a potentially dismal life – a life that I could now put behind me. My family were happy and my life was shaping up nicely.

Cas and I began to make plans to get married. The first date we had in mind had to be changed because it clashed with a World Cup football match so, eventually, we decided to tie the knot at Clacton Methodist Church on May 25, 1985.

Having started his career as an assistant manager at McDonald's Kensington High Street restaurant, Cas was quickly promoted to store manager. Cas had a thirst for knowledge and it was of no surprise that he wanted to progress as far as possible within the organisation.

Life at Kensington had not been uneventful though. One day the store had been raided by gunmen and all the staff had been locked in the freezer. They were only released after Cas had handed over the day's takings.

McDonald's were introducing a franchising system and this very much interested Cas. He applied, and was accepted, as a graduate at the McDonald's Hamburger University in East Finchley – and yes, it really does exist! This is an exclusive institution where only eight of every 1,000 students are accepted compared to the 18% acceptance rate at Oxford University and 20.8% acceptance rate at Cambridge *(based on 2019 figures)*.

With Cas now working at East Finchley and me continuing my nursing career in Colchester, we did not see an awful lot of each other – and this was a situation that would endure for many years, our respective roles throughout our married life ensuring we spent a lot of time apart. For me, though, this was rarely a problem.

Having spent his time at the Hamburger University learning about all aspects of McDonald's training schemes, franchising and management systems within the company's business, Cas became a franchising consultant. This huge step-up in his career was to sometimes see him disappear for weeks on end on trips across Europe. Of course, for many couples, this could have posed a severe strain on their relationship. We were fortunate that it didn't for us.

Cas's meteoric career progression also saw a dramatic increase in his income, allowing us to buy our first house in Colchester.

Our first son Daniel was born in 1986, James followed in 1989. It was shortly after, when James was only four months old that Peggy, Cas's mum, suffered a fatal heart attack. This was a terribly sad time for the family.

The arrival of our boys meant I put my nursing career on hold. I had been working in hospitals in Colchester, Clacton and London. I spent the next 12 years studying to gain further qualifications and was so delighted to have gained a Bsc Hons in Health and Social Care in my forties.

I was fortunate enough to be a 'stay at home' mum, a 'job' that I loved. I still say that raising my children to be the kind, caring adults they have become is my biggest achievement in life.

Cas, however, was driven by his career to such a degree that he was rarely at home and he saw very little of the boys other than time spent taking family holidays and the odd weekend off. At one time I even began to work at McDonald's in order to spend a little more time with Cas but, to be honest, I just didn't have the patience to deal with some of the more difficult customers.

In 1991 we moved house again, this time to Marks Tey on the outskirts of Colchester then, in 1996, our third son Stephen was born. Also that year the opportunity arose for Cas and I to take on the franchises of three McDonald's restaurants in Colchester – one in the town's High Street, another in Cowdray Avenue and a further restaurant on the outskirts of town at the Tollgate Retail Park.

In 1998 we moved house again, this time back into Colchester into an impressive property on the Shrub End Road which was to be our forever family home. We always appreciated what we had and we loved this house, often saying how lucky we were to have found it.

Cas was often away attending various training seminars, conferences and visiting other franchised restaurants. Sometimes I was lucky enough to go with him. If he wasn't away, he would work very long hours, usually including at weekends. He would get up at six in the morning and not get home until late at night. There was always a daily phone call to the restaurants first thing in the morning and last thing at night, even when we were on holiday! This would be to hear the figures of the day, such as how much money was taken per hour. The boys always remembered him doing this!

Long days and long hours meant it was tough for us and the boys, but despite the long absences, we were happy. Cas had McDonald's and I had the boys!

We were fortunate enough to be able to afford some marvellous holidays. Once we all went to Australia. On arrival we hired a large motor home and had a wonderful time. We all learnt to ski and had yearly skiing holidays. James later worked in Canada as a snowboarding instructor as he had truly got the bug so we enjoyed a few trips to Canada to ski as a family.

When Cas retired, I surprised him by booking an all-inclusive holiday in Mexico for the whole family. It was the holiday of a lifetime, and one that none of us will ever forget. A surprise retirement party was also arranged.

Decision making

While Cas's work ethic was deeply engrained there was one rule of McDonald's he could not agree with. The company had ruled that no-one under the age of 17 could be employed by any of its franchisees.

Cas could not see any reason for this. As far as he was concerned, any youngster from the age of 15 should be given the opportunity to earn a little money of their own. All our own boys had worked shifts at our restaurants before they reached the age of 17.

Yet despite Cas's high standing in the company and his undeniable expertise within the franchising and training areas of the business, it all meant very little to the big chiefs at McDonalds. His standing as a franchisee was decided.

Our future was about to be changed; the hiring of 'the under-aged' would result in the 'blotting of his copybook'. We were soon to learn that the renewing of the franchise contracts on two of our three restaurants was to be denied. We were not given the option to extend the contract by a further 20 years.

Although we still had five years to run on one of our restaurants, there was the option to sell all three. With no appeal available, our fate was sealed. So, after 38 years, the relationship with McDonalds ended. I was gutted for Cas as he had dedicated so much of his life to McDonalds and was a true ambassador to the brand.

I will never forget the day he told me that the company had refused to renew his contract. Cas, who rarely expressed sad emotions, was broken, devastated. We both felt that McDonalds were recruiting younger franchisees and had their sights on our restaurants for someone new. Our time was done. My respect for McDonalds went and never returned. I cannot deny that we were blessed financially because of McDonalds but we had sacrificed a lot of family time in the process.

To say there was uproar from other franchisees in the UK and across Europe was an understatement. Many were furious and many letters of complaints were sent to McDonalds' head office. This changed nothing. His long, distinguished union with the company was over.

This had never been the way Cas had imagined ending his association with McDonalds but he was not bitter. Instead, he saw it as an amazing opportunity to do something else. In true Cas style he would simply say 'It is what it is'.

The positives were that we were able to see our boys through university without them incurring any debts, our home was paid for, and we felt, for sure, that we would be okay. We decided to invest and purchased a number of properties to lease out to students and we purchased a city centre flat in Liverpool.

Very quickly, future planning began. Cas intended to enjoy life and to embrace all of his interests. He was a life-long fan of Rugby Union side Wasps and he was fascinated in other cultures, particularly Chinese and Indian, and in Indian monasteries. He was also into mysticism and had many books on these subjects.

As previously mentioned, Cas had many books about the American philosopher/author Dale Carnegie. He studied the subject for many years and I would say that this is what inspired his positive mental attitude. He would often use quotations from some of the books, applying them to everything he did.

'Fill your mind with thoughts of peace, courage, health and hope'

'Count your blessings, not your troubles'

'Decide how much anxiety a thing may be worth and refuse to give it more'

'Remember today is the tomorrow you worried about yesterday'

'Our thoughts make us what we are'

'Today is our most precious possession. It is our only possession'

These quotations and more would prove to be my platform to recovery.
Cas particularly loved Chinese proverbs and was a great believer in the principle of 'Only you can make things better, only you can change it.' He was only interested in positive vibes. I could come home from work and tell him I'd had a terrible day and he would ask: 'Was it *really* that bad?' Or I might have said about something along the lines of: 'Oh I really hated that,' and he'd just say: 'Well, hate is a really strong word isn't it?'
If I were to say 'That's the worst thing that could happen,' he would reply, 'Is it? Is it *really*?' These responses at a time when I was feeling irritable were rather annoying and, I felt, somewhat condescending.
Cas practised Tai Chi for many years and at one point he considered becoming an instructor. He had many books on the subject. He was considering returning to this practise as he had more time on his hands. We were warming to the idea of retirement.
Most days we would sit down on our patio and have a cup of coffee at around 11 o'clock. We admired the garden, our surroundings and often expressed our appreciation of what we had. We would often chat about the boys, our grandchildren, and we made plans and talked about our fitness regimes – and even life and death.
Regarding death, Cas was always blasé. He used to say 'you can't change it, so just accept the fate that is already determined.' I remember thinking that it's a good job that we cannot see into the future.
Yes, Cas was a glass full sort of person while I was definitely in the glass half empty category. I guess he was Ying and I was Yang. We had very opposite attitudes and opinions about

all aspects of life. Attitudes and opinions that had transpired from our different life experiences, education and family connections.

He believed passionately in alternative and holistic practises but, because of my medical training, I believed in the scientific approach; we rarely agreed on these topics, our mindsets were complete opposites.

–o0o–

'You can't change it, you've been given so many heartbeats and, when your time is up, that's it'
Cas Morehen

–o0o–

Cas had a lifelong interest in hypnotherapy. He had studied this alongside McDonalds. He also studied Neuro-Linguistic Programming (NLP) which is an approach to communication, personal development and psychotherapy. It is believed that NLP can treat problems such as phobias, depression, allergies and learning disorders. He revisited his studies and started an Open University course in psychotherapy. Alongside this, he practised hypnotherapy, helping many friends and some family members.

Health-wise, Cas was in pretty good shape, this despite having had a hip realignment operation. He also had Keratoconus, a non-inflammatory eye condition which required him to have occasional operations to improve his vision.

Cas also suffered from Lone AF (atrial fibrillation), a heart condition that would cause his heart to stop momentarily and then race to catch up. He was prescribed tablets to combat this. We were reassured that this was not a life-threatening condition and he continued to be monitored yearly, getting the reassurance in April 2018 that 'all was well'.

Obviously, Cas had not been too concerned about this condition as, with more time on his hands, he discovered cycling! He became obsessed with it and would sometimes want to ride up to 80 miles a day! Worse still, he wanted me to join him. So I got a decent bike and off we went.
Whilst I enjoyed this, I also liked to spend time tending the garden and often it became a battle of wills as to what I would be doing – cycling or gardening.
Whenever Cas decided to do anything it was always full-on, he would give it one hundred percent. It was never enough to cycle 80 miles – he had to do it within a particular time. We'd go out for bike rides and when we came back we would compare our heartbeats and calories lost. We'd compare the times we'd taken to cycle up certain hills.
Cas was so competitive that he would never willingly allow me to overtake him on a hill, but sometimes, when I did, I would stick my tongue out at him as I passed and that would be enough to spur him on to pass me again a couple of seconds later.
We entered the London Prudential – a 100-mile cycle challenge on the streets of London. To qualify to complete the whole course, we needed to reach the 46-miles point by a certain time. On the day things were going really well for us. We were making good time until we stopped to use the toilet. That was costly because we arrived at the 46-mile point two minutes late. We had misjudged our timing and were really disappointed not to have had the chance to complete the 100. But we vowed to re-enter the next year. This, as it turned out, was not to be.
Cas couldn't do small talk which may have led some people to see him as being unsociable. It was sometimes hard to get a conversation out of him. If ever he was asked a question or for an opinion on something, he would think carefully, maybe stroke his chin, and sometimes it could be several seconds before he responded.
He joined the Rotary Club and rose to be appointed president within two years in 2018. He adored being part of Rotary

(forum) where he would socialise amongst like-minded people. I too enjoyed the company of the Rotarian ladies and it proved to be a new lease of socialising for both of us.

We were so different to each other, ying and yang. I was an extrovert, especially if a dance floor was available, yet simplistic. Cas was far more comfortable sitting quietly in the background. Yet, over the years, and in particular amongst the Rotarians, he gradually became a little more outward looking, while his calming attitude may have begun to have influenced me a little more.

I guess our relationship could have been described as one of contentment, respect and adoring love. A bond that had developed between two very different people – different in a way that we enjoyed our own interests, had different sets of friends and often did our own thing. This independence would prove to be my saving grace.

The bubble bursts

At 53 years old I had experienced the death of my grandma who was 87. I had lost no other members of my family or close friends. This was to drastically change over the next five years. Two dear friends were lost to cancer, as was my brother. I then lost my dad when he was 85. Every family will, at some time, experience the loss of a loved one and ours was no exception.

Cas was just 12 years old when his father passed away and, when he was 40, he lost his mother too, both parents succumbing to cardiac problems. Then, in 2016, Cas's twin sister Christine (Chris) was diagnosed with cancer and passed away at the end of 2017.

Cas was pragmatic over the loss of his sister and parents – not that he didn't care, of course he did, but his firm belief that we are all built up of molecules and atoms convinced him that they were all still with us in the form of energy – an energy that never dies.

As a result, Cas did not grieve in the same way that most others would. 'It is what it is,' he said, 'the time was right.' Cas would say 'When my turn comes, I want to go out like a light.'

I was just a practical, simple person who had to have evidence of a continued existence. As a nurse I had been scientifically trained. I have never been convinced there is a god. I remember saying to my nan just before she died, 'please come back and tell me where you are', yet I still haven't heard anything.

The passing of my friends had been harrowing to witness. Linda succumbed to breast cancer. To be honest, her death came as a relief, she had suffered enough for 24 years!

Jill had recently lost her daughter and, when she also became unwell, she told me she would be reunited with her daughter. While saddened by her death, I could at least comfort myself that Jill's wish had, hopefully, come true.

My brother Martin died in 2015 from throat cancer. It was sad, obviously, although I was sadder for my mum as she'd lost a child and the dynamics of our family had been changed forever.

Looking back at these bereavements of my friends and relatives I realise now I had managed to cope pretty well on an emotional level because, in most cases, their deaths had been expected and had proved to be merciful releases from long periods of illness and pain or, in my dad's case, mental anguish.

Not one of their deaths affected me the way the next one would.

-0-

On Saturday, October 20, 2018 I was booked into hospital in Colchester for a sinus operation. On the Friday night beforehand I'd said goodbye to Cas and our oldest son Daniel in Southend. We had been looking after the grandchildren during the day. Cas and Daniel had planned to go to a beer festival that evening. The following day, joined by my grandson Jack and my other son Stephen, they planned to head off to the Wasps rugby match.

When I got home I prepared myself for my surgery the following morning. Later that evening I got a text from Cas asking what time he should pick me up from the hospital. I texted back to tell him not to worry, that he should have a lie in. Cas texted back 'Okay', and, though I didn't know it at the time, that was to be the last text I would ever receive from him.

After leaving the beer festival, Cas spent the night at Daniel's in Southend and on the Saturday morning they drove to Coventry to watch the Wasps play rugby, returning later that evening. The journey back to Colchester followed, arriving approximately at half past eight. Daniel and the others headed back to Southend. What happened during that evening is unknown.

I never heard back from Cas regarding my discharge from hospital. I arranged for a friend to drive me home. I had an uneasy feeling that Cas had been in an accident while out cycling. This was not the case, it was far worse!
On entry to the house I sensed all was not as it should be. It appeared that a catastrophic fatal cardiac arrest had occurred. It was evident that Cas had been making a cup of tea at the time, just as his mum had done when she suffered her fatal heart attack all those years before.
An ambulance was called, also the police. My friend Yanna arrived and immediately she set about contacting everybody, including our boys as I was in such a dreadful state. The real state of my mind would be evident by entries in my journal.
I found myself in the lounge, rocking in grief and asking over and over again, what am I going to do? How am I going to cope? And . . . 'I can't be on my own'. Even at this point I just knew I couldn't be on my own for the rest of my life, I was far too young. That must have sounded so callous.
With the police present because of an unexpected death, and the ambulance crews arriving, the house was filling up, and then the neighbours came in too. To be honest, at the time, I didn't want any of the constant intrusion.
People were trying to console me, trying to talk me through things, but nothing made sense. I just wasn't hearing what people were telling me, nor did I want to hear it.
I was in a dreadful state but, thankfully, my boys and their partners were brilliant. All took on their own roles of organising, sorting and caring for me. They spent every hour, every minute, doing their utmost to support me in every way possible. I just wanted to curl up into the foetal position and die, I literally did want to die at that point.
My God, how would I have got through those days without them? Despite the pain they were going through themselves, they were doing everything they could to help me cope with mine.

Eventually, as they had our little grandsons Harrison and Jack to care for, Daniel and Carrie returned to their home in Southend, leaving the others to remain with me.

The following week I too went to stay in Southend with Daniel and Carrie. They looked after me well but it was a constant reminder of what I was missing. I just couldn't stay there.

I guess I was jealous. I was angry with myself for feeling that way, but I just couldn't help it. I didn't just want Cas back – I wanted back the entire 33 years we'd had together, including the boys young again. Nothing less than that would have sufficed.

I returned home. The quiet, stillness of the house was awful. The TV and radio were put on high volume – this was to become routine when entering the house and as soon as I woke up. There was a constant flow of flowers but all were immediately put in the bin and the cards put away in a cupboard without reading. Why was it that people thought that flowers and a few words in a card could possibly help me in any way?

Stephen stayed with me for ages. He tended to my facial bandages, fed me ham sandwiches and Bakewell tarts. He ensured that I took pain killers and antibiotics. He stroked my brow as I tried to sleep. My youngest son had become my nurse; the roles had been reversed. I will forever be grateful for his strength, his words of comfort and simply just being there.

I needed reassurance that life could go on, that everything would, one day, be alright. It was reasonable to me that those that could best help me, reassure me, would be other widows or widowers. Those with near perfect lives would be no use to me whatsoever – whoever they were.

I decided to re-connect with some friends who I knew had been widowed, one recently, the other a few years previously. Both were able to offer me an insight into how this new, unwanted journey would progress.

And so, it came to be that during the next few months, I would surround myself with widows – local widow groups, online widow forums. Only they would truly understand my raw grief. Only they were qualified to offer me advice about the way forward, to support me during the darkest of days. I would credit these women with providing me with the encouragement and strength to carry on.

–o0o–

'Some days I feel as if I'm conquering the world in your honour; and some days I feel as if I'm lost in the heartache of your absence.'
Unknown

–o0o–

The subsequent post-mortem revealed that the cause of Cas's death was a catastrophic cardiac arrest. I was informed that even if a paramedic had been with Cas at the time he had collapsed there would have been no chance of saving him. I never read the report and still haven't. My biggest fear is that I would read something different – that, had I been there, the outcome may have been different.

For that, at least, I was grateful because he wouldn't have known anything about it. Throughout his life he had played his cards very well. His final card had been played just as he had wanted it – to go out like a light. That is the only aspect of his ordeal that I am grateful for.

It seems that, having got home from the rugby, Cas had watched the game on television which had been recorded. And then, as per usual, at somewhere between 10 and 11 o'clock, he'd gone into the kitchen to make a cup of tea and to eat some chocolate. The teabag was still in the cup.

I spent the days in bed, my mind in a turmoil. I continued to eat very little and I had serious doubts about the path that my future would take or if I even wanted a future. The dark thoughts, dislike of everything and everyone were at the forefront of my mind. I felt that I had become someone different, someone that I did not recognise or even like.

DAYS 1-5 (from my journal)

'Hell, devastated, crushed. I cannot understand why. I can't breathe.'
'So, so angry that he has left me.'
'Cannot be on my own.'
'Silent screaming, loud screaming, followed by shaking.'
'Random palpitations, panic attacks and pacing the floor.'
'I hate everyone, go away, I hate you all for being alive.'

I started walking and began to process life as I now knew it. This was just the beginning of what was to be the toughest journey of my life but the torment of mixed emotions would always return. I was still experiencing what I can only describe as a dark veil which enveloped me at a similar time each day – usually around three o'clock – a veil which usually saw me having palpitations, feeling panicky and repeatedly saying 'oh my God, I can't do this, I don't want to do this.'

DAY 15 (from my journal)

'Poor Daniel, having to listen to me whilst driving (trip to Peterborough).'

'Felt sick in the pit of my stomach, why me? It's unfair that my family has been torn apart.'

'Stop talking about your family.' Does he not realise that I want what he has, my life, my starting out on life's journey?'

'I just want to disappear, tell no one where I am.'

The boys and I decided to get a tattoo. We chose transcript's from greetings cards that Cas had written. The words – his handwriting – were tattooed onto us – quite a painful experience.

Also, the 'lightning bolt' attributed to the singer David Bowie (Cas's favourite singer) was chosen by Stephen and tattooed onto his ankle. It was our way of ensuring that he will always be with us.

Feeling vulnerable

GRIEF affects people in many different ways. Some people may question their faith – asking where God had been when all this was going on. Others may experience anger that someone has died suddenly and that they didn't get the chance to say goodbye, while some may regret something that was, or was not, said.

Of course, not all relationships are perfect, even good. If a person has been living under the shadow of their partner or spouse, or has maybe been unhappy in their relationship, there could be a feeling of release and that, in its own way, can lead to feelings of guilt. I've since met widows who had been almost ruled by controlling husbands/partners, and others who have spent years caring for those who have been terminally ill.

It is quite understandable, in some cases, that a bereavement can also be viewed as an opportunity to experience a new-found freedom, the chance to move forward in life and to have more control over their own futures.

If you love hard, you lose hard. If you believe your marriage or relationship was good, as you wanted, your loss will be even more keenly felt.

I noticed that some people would express insensitive comments, such as 'well at least you were loved for 33 years, some people never experienced that'. I couldn't stand comments like that! At the beginning, I could not come to terms with this concept. If you have had the best, why should it end? Are we only given so many years to be happy then?

DAY SIX AND BEYOND (From my journal)

'Why has their marriage survived, they don't even love each other? She had an affair.'
'I used to enjoy helping at the homeless soup kitchen, hate it now. What do homeless people give to society? They are not even healthy, yet they are alive, how is that fair?'

I had not only lost the love of my life, but also lost me as a one half of a couple, our future, our everything. I had always been an enthusiastic person, taking pleasure from the simple things in life. I now felt no pleasure in anything at all. I felt no drive to get anything done, to shower, dress, cook, shop or to do housework. Who was there to do it for or even see it?

(From my journal)
'What's the point?'

I felt a strong urge to find a new identity, create a new person that would now have to tackle life her way. I accepted that the new way was going to be totally different to what I had been used to.

(From my journal
'Today I've decided to do a massive friendship cull. Those that are of no use to me, who bring nothing to the table, are gone.'

I did exactly that. I emailed many friends and relatives and explained my intentions:

'Please understand that I cannot be around you at the moment, certainly not as one half of a couple that you used to socialise with. I know that you all mean well but I cannot stand your empty platitudes and trait comments. Some comments are meaningless and insensitive to hear.
'I am also struggling to hear/see about your perfect lives when mine has been shattered. I worry that I will say cruel, bitter things to you that I will certainly regret.
'For these reasons I would like to be left alone, not contacted. What I need to do is be like a caterpillar. The caterpillar goes into its cocoon and in time emerges as a butterfly. I will make contact when I emerge.'

I eventually emerged and made some contact, but not with everyone. Some friends are now in that past and there is no intention to reunite with any of them. I had reduced the time spent with my boys, mum and grandchildren – I just couldn't face family stuff. Those occasions only reminded me that we were not a complete unit any more, a fact that I hated being reminded of.

I had also started to compare my boys' grief to mine. Mine was surely worse? They had lost a parent, which is in the right order in the circle of life. Their plans, future were still there. I had lost a life partner, all our plans and our future. I felt anxious that my irrational mind would say these things to the boys. I would have been so sad, disappointed and heartbroken to have upset them.

–o0o–

'Every day may not be a good day but there is good in every day'

Unknown

–o0o–

Fear is a natural feeling; a feeling that is emphasised by the loss of a loved one. Being alone at night with no-one to talk to can be very nerve-racking. I would advise taking small steps, taking one challenge at a time at a pace to suit yourself. Prioritise what needs to be done and, if possible, surround yourself with people who can offer practical help. Only surround yourself with positive people. Negativity serves no purpose at all.

Be selfish, only do what you want to do. I was concerned that, now I was on my own, I might be overlooked with social invites. 'You won't leave me out, will you?' I'd asked, and they all reassured me they wouldn't. Then, later, when the offers came, I didn't always want to go because they were all couples. Then I would worry they wouldn't invite me again. It was a confusing time for my friends who had previously been told to make no contact with me!

Some days my grief is more hidden in the background and I barely realise its existence. Other days, it is more apparent, particularly any days I spend with my boys and grandchildren. Sometimes I even wondered if I didn't have children, whether my grief might be easier to cope with. I just look at my boys and feel so sorry for them. I feel that I cannot exhibit signs of sadness because they will see it and be pitiful towards me. I can't stand pity in any form.

If I just had me to think about, I could draw a line under this period of my life and do what I need to do for me and no-one else. Yet a widow who has no family will say how lucky I am to have family. They simply do not realise that for every milestone that I should have enjoyed with Cas by my side, I am now alone, and it hurts like mad. BUT of course, I also know how lucky I am to have my boys, the gratitude returned to me very quickly.

I find myself working out how many milestones there are still to come – engagements, weddings, babies – the list is endless. I have also worked out in how many more years these milestones are likely to occur. If these milestones are in five or more years, my recovery progression will be further advanced and I will be able to cope better. Is this crazy thinking?

People constantly told me that the first year would be the worst. I hated them saying that. It was as if, after a year, the grief would subside and life would be good. Unless one has experienced the loss of a loved one, he/she will never understand the devastation that is felt. For some these feelings can last for years, sometimes a lifetime. I hung on those words to the point that I ticked off the weeks, months and, indeed, the year mark on the 2019 calendar.

It is important to realise that you are not necessarily the only person grieving and, sometimes, other people's way of coping with loss could be very different to your own and this should be respected. Some people want to talk about their loss constantly, others not at all.

Personally, I choose not to talk about Cas too much. It's too painful. Also, I dread meeting up with people whose first words are 'I'm so sorry to hear about Cas.' They are only 'sorry' in that moment. They go back to their blessed lives and are unlikely to give it another thought. I just can't deal with that, even though I know they mean well. What is it that they would like you to respond with?

Hopefully, at some time in the future, I will be able to deal with situations like that in a better way. I do ask myself if I too had once offered insincere sounding remarks before I had experienced such a devastating loss.

Some people become very insular – they cannot see joy in anything. I used to get so much pleasure looking at the first autumn leaves. What a beautiful sight! Now, however, such natural wonders don't mean an awful lot to me. I really do hope that such simple pleasures return.

(From my journal)
'James is home. Walked into town with friend Sue. I cannot cope with seeing couples together, doing normal things. Why are they allowed? Oh well, their time will come.'

–o0o–

'Look for something positive in each day even if some days you have to look a little harder'
Unknown

–o0o–

Sometimes, when I think I have managed to be more positive, my anger can resurface. For example, if I notice someone who is puffing away at a cigarette – well, that makes me so angry. Why can they not value their life more – have they no respect for their body? Do they not appreciate how precious life is?

Practicalities

I'm a very practical person and, almost immediately, I began to try to sort things out.
Within a couple of weeks of Cas's death I had cleared out his office. It was absolutely full of stuff which I had often moaned about. I will forever hold the memory of the boys filling a carrier bag each of keepsakes – it broke my heart to see that. As for our bedroom and bathroom, almost everything belonging to Cas had been packed up and removed within a month. For me, this was not a minute too soon and I have no regrets whatsoever.
All of his clothes were disposed of, given to charity, with the exception of one dressing gown, a coat and a sweatshirt. These I rolled up into a ball, like a pillow which I would cuddle up to and even talk to when I went to bed each night for several weeks.
Fortunately, as time passed, that came out of the bed and went into the drawer underneath and now, it is stored in a black bag in the loft. There does not seem any purpose to keeping these items other than my boys will find them when I've gone and gain some comfort in the knowledge that I kept them.
Life seemed so dark, so hopeless. I began to feel as if I was at the bottom of a dark hole, not unlike that in one of those spiral coin collectors. I imagined myself at the bottom of the spiral, desperately trying to crawl my way back up to the top. After a struggle I would almost manage to grip the top of the spiral with my fingertips before another penny would roll down and knock me back down to the bottom again.
That penny would normally be in the form of yet another 'well wisher' giving me their words of wisdom that held absolutely no credibility – how could it? They had no idea of my trauma unless they had walked in my shoes.
With my mind in a turmoil I began frantically trying to sort out my new, unplanned life. I did all sorts of ridiculous things. I spent hours researching new jobs all over the country, hours

researching trips and world cruises, jobs abroad, new hobbies, walking groups, meet-up groups, widows' groups and organisations such as Age Concern and dog walking.

Daniel and I embarked on researching property investment. I needed a purpose; a direction, and this project gave me that, but only for a short time. The dark veil continued to engulf me at random times leaving me helpless, vulnerable and scared for my future.

I desperately needed positivity around me and my sons all took on different roles. Daniel took charge of all the finances, contacting banks and shutting down the various computer accounts and so on, while James, who oozes positivity, began advising me what I should be doing. As mentioned, Stephen became my nurse/carer.

I remember vividly asking Stephen on the 10th day, who'd been feeding me. When he told me it was him and what he had been giving me, I couldn't recall that at all. In just a few days I'd lost a huge amount of weight. I was very fortunate to have had such good support over those 10 days and beyond.

I was fortunate to have had Lou, the daughter of my friend Ailsa, stay with me twice a week while she attended Essex University. She gave me a purpose to get up, clean the house and cook. She was a great source of comfort and companionship that I will be forever grateful for.

Tom – Daniel's friend – who is like a fourth son to me, was and still is using one of the garages to keep his garden equipment in. He too offered huge support and was a crucial link to check on how my boys were through regular Whatsapp communications. He was also able to update the boys on how I was as he saw me most days. I was so grateful for this link and I know that the boys were too.

Saying goodbye

We began to organise Cas's funeral. We set the date, November 14, the music and the eulogy. We got in touch with the celebrant and organised what you might call a Humanist service. I knew exactly what music to choose.

Cas had a white coffin emblazoned with the symbols of three major events of his life. On one side was the double golden arches of McDonald's, on the other, the England rugby rose emblem and, on another side, the honour badge of The Rotary Club of which Cas was the president of our local branch.

It was during this week that I first heard the sound of a tin whistle. I recorded the following in my journal:

'Whilst writing down more ideas, I heard the faint sound of the tin whistle. The two notes that I heard were the only two that Cas had learnt to play. I heard two notes, four times gradually fading out. Could it be that it has taken until now for his spirit to transition to its final resting place and this was goodbye?'

We didn't create a normal order of service, choosing instead to provide a print-out of Cas's life with pictures because, we felt, this pushed forward the positive attitude that had been so important to him in life. The theme of the eulogy, read brilliantly by James, was based on Cas's belief – 'this has happened, it is what it is, so now let's just get on with it'.

And that's just what we, as a family, have tried to do. James for instance, who is a doctor in Sports Science and nutrition, told me that there were three of life's boxes that I needed to sort out and that I could control, the first one by concentrating on regaining my health and well-being. The second box concerned my emotional healing and the third, dealing with heartbreak and loneliness.

It was like Cas was standing in front of me saying 'it's shit, it's happened, this is what you've got to do.'

Fired by his advice, eight weeks after Cas's death I flew to Denmark on a trip that Cas and I had originally booked up with the intention of us travelling together. We had intended to visit James's future mother-in-law. We had planned for James and his fiancée Nura to meet us at the airport and then to just turn up Nura's mum's home to surprise her on her birthday.

–o0o–

'Start by doing what is necessary; then do what's possible; and suddenly you are doing the impossible'
Francis of Assissi

–o0o–

On the way to Stansted airport I remember listening to the song 'I want to break free' by Queen playing on the car radio. Suddenly I can REALLY hear the joyful sound of music again. The words of the last verse felt so strong, so positive, that it became a light bulb moment for me:

'But life still goes on;
I can't get used to living without, living without,
living without you by my side;
I don't want to live alone;
hey, God knows, got to make it on my own;
so baby can't you see – I've got to break free'.
(Credit: Lyrics by John Deacon)

It had been daunting travelling by myself to Stansted. First of all I entered the wrong car park, which totally panicked me, then, having checked in, I realised I had the wrong-sized suitcase with me which cost me an extra £40.
It was awful being on the plane surrounded by couples which just served to remind me, if ever that was needed, that I was on

my own. To pass the time I decided to read a book and that helped to take my mind of it.

On arrival in Denmark, everyone was so friendly and cheerful, and I was being spoiled by their hospitality and being offered all sorts of food and drink. Nura's mother was very kind and, the following day, she was keen to show me around Copenhagen though, to be honest, I was not in the right frame of mind to enjoy the sights. I was feeling numb and vague and didn't really take anything in.

The next day, although having slept well, I woke up feeling as if I was about to break down. Everything had become a bit too much. I became overwhelmed by it all so I sneaked off to my bedroom where I curled up into a foetal position and cried my eyes out and that's how James eventually found me. He was so good, comforting me as I sobbed inconsolably.

–o0o–

'It takes strength to make your way through grief, to grab hold of life and to let it pull you forward'
Patti Davis

–o0o–

James later told me that seeing me in that state had reminded him of a David Attenborough programme he had seen that featured a baby elephant mourning the death of its mother. Having heard that I vowed I would never let any of my boys see me in that state again – and I never again wanted to be compared to a baby elephant! I believe though that that moment proved to be a key point in determining that I should do my best to get my life back together as soon as possible.

While in Denmark I decided to go to a café in Copenhagen to meet Orjan, the widower of my best friend Linda. Linda had died of breast cancer and brain tumours four years earlier. Orjan lived and worked in Malmo in Sweden which is just over the bridge from Denmark. Orjan spent a long time in the café comforting me and relating his own journey through grief to the point where he was at the time.

Orjan is a dear friend and our chat really helped me. I made him a promise that, a year on, I would return to that café to meet him again so he could see for himself how far I had progressed in my own journey.

While James, Nura and I were on a train in Denmark, we all looked in disbelief when we saw a young girl wearing a hat that showed the Wasps' symbol of the Coventry-based rugby team. This was Cas's favourite team. He saw them play on the Saturday before tragedy struck. We all felt that this was a sign that he was somehow 'with us'.

An entry from my journal:

'Feeling strangely positive, next year I shall join walking groups, charity groups, be a dog sitter, start a gardening business, set up a bereavement help group in a motor home called 'healing on wheels'. Yep, I'll be the one to help all others, my new purpose in life. The boys will be pleased.'

Later that day, I added the following;

'Nothing will change. I will remain heartbroken, empty and have no purpose in life. Every day I wake up on my own, plan a solitary day. The knife is so embedded in my heart it actually hurts. I feel real pain in my chest.'

The following morning this was added:

'I had the weirdest of dreams! I dreamt that I was on a train. A cleaner told me that she had found a pile of clothes neatly folded and left on the chair. No-one ever claimed them as their own. Was that Cas making his final exit, saying goodbye? Very bizarre thought!'

From darkness to light

THE following pages will illustrate the dark and malevolent thoughts that can sometimes surface following the loss of a loved one.

Admittedly, these are on the more extreme side of the scale but, nevertheless, I now realise that, as these thoughts were racing around my head, I was not actually going mad – other people have experienced similar emotions too, it's just that most people do not express them so openly as I did.

By nature I am an empathetic, caring person. I am a nurse by profession so at no time had I ever wished people dead or that they would to come to harm. But my grief had turned me into a bitter person, bitter that other people were surviving, particularly if they were not looking after themselves, or if they had been fortunate enough to reach old age.

This was particularly so if they were couples – that would be the spectre of jealously rearing its ugly head – why couldn't that be me and Cas?

I have belonged to several bereavement groups since Cas died and, in each of them, I have met several people who have admitted quietly to me that they have, at some time or another, also had these awful thoughts.

I am hoping that readers who, it can be reasonable to assume, are going through the grieving process themselves at this moment, will understand how I was feeling. There is a good chance they may be experiencing similar thoughts themselves from time to time and, therefore, I hope they will not judge me or pass judgement for opening up about the more extreme emotions I have experienced as I have been trying to rebuild my life.

Those months really changed my character. I have realised that some of my more extreme thoughts – for instance wishing something bad will happen to someone else – was not really what I wanted to happen at all.

When I returned to work in the nursing home I was responsible for looking after many very elderly and sick people and at no point did I ever wish them to come to any harm.
It was as if I had a totally different personality whilst at work. I was the old Julie there – that was a different aspect of my life and a time when I had to think more about the needs and feelings of others rather than my own.
Working in the nursing home gave me a totally different perspective on life. It was only when I was not in a working environment that those awful feelings would engulf me – it was jealousy, bitterness – why should they be happy when I feel like this? You might be happy now, I would think, but your time will come. Someday *you* will feel as bad as I am feeling right now.

–o0o–

'A positive attitude causes a chain reaction of positive thoughts, events and outcomes. It is a catalyst and it sparks extraordinary results'
Wade Boggs

–o0o–

My 83-year-old mother scolded me about my feelings one day. 'That's not a very nice thing to say,' she said, 'that just isn't you.' She was right but, at the time I'd blurted it out, it had made me feel better.
Within weeks of losing Cas, I already knew that I could not spend another 25 to 30 years on my own. Certainly not living alone. I missed him terribly and I experienced a wide range of emotions. Loneliness was at the forefront, obviously sadness. I thought about who could come and live with me? My mum? Friends? Anybody would do! It was ridiculous, unrealistic thinking.

So many people tried to comfort me but I just wasn't having any of it. I could not stand pity and I pushed so many well-meaning people away.

Looking back, some of those thoughts were really unpleasant. I was wishing other women would lose their husbands and I was not allowing my sister to send a text to her husband in front of me – or even to mention his name.

I decided I wanted to help the homeless, as I had done previously by serving the soup. I thought that this task would make me feel grateful for what I had, help those less fortunate. However, I had an overwhelming urge to see them all come to harm – after all, what was their worth in the world whereas Cas had had so much to give? What a terrible thing to think! It didn't seem terrible at that time.

I couldn't see any of our friends without feeling jealous that they still had their husbands – especially if they hadn't been in touch with me but, in their defence, that's probably because in my grief I'd told them to leave me alone.

To be honest, despite the progress I have made, I still sometimes feel like that today.

On my really dark days I would think of crashing my car so that I would go into a coma and not have to think about anything any more. At times I didn't want to see my sister, or my boys. I just wanted to disappear.

Jeanette, my sister, persuaded me to go with her to a holiday centre as we usually did every November. During the drive to Norfolk I was bending her ears about my latest silly plans.

To her credit she just went along with it all. 'Yes, yes,' she'd say, probably wondering at the same time what I was going on about. She knew that every plan I came up with would probably not go any further so she just let me ramble on and on.

At the holiday centre there were a lot of older couples – and that didn't go down well with me. I just couldn't bear seeing them enjoying themselves and holding each other's hands. Why are they still alive? Why have they had 60 or more years together?

Eventually Jeanette said: 'Julie, you need to really look at those couples. Look at that couple over there – what do you think?'
I replied: 'A happily married couple.'
'Well,' she replied: 'I don't necessarily see that. I see a couple that might have come away for the weekend that may have marriage problems.
'As for that couple over there, I see a couple who may have come away for a break having had a diagnosis of something like cancer.
'Maybe that couple over there have been remarried having both lost their partners, maybe that couple have just lost a child.'
Her words made me think that life may appear rosy, but many people are experiencing a form of anguish – I am not the only one! Also that if I can't see other people's grief, then they can't see mine. People would not be looking at me feeling pity. Realising this was an enormous thing for me. I felt considerably better about seeing couples together and realised that they had every right to share things together.
A few years before Cas had joined the Rotary Club in Colchester and, in June 2018, he became the club's president. At the time of his death, Cas had been halfway through his term in the role.
The Rotarians decided that, although Cas had passed away, they still wanted to honour his presidential year in his absence so, instead of appointing a new president, he was kept on as president for the following year. I found this very hard because, in every newsletter, there were stories about Cas alongside pictures of him. At every fundraising event there were tributes to him.
Then I was approached by committee members – could they instal a defibrillator with a plaque in his memory at the town hall? By now I was receiving so many telephone calls following each tribute to Cas that I was struggling more than ever to come to terms with his death.

I decided that having a defibrillator and plaque in his honour would serve to increase those calls and it was not something I felt I could cope with. Besides, I thought, a defibrillator wouldn't have helped save Cas's life. I agreed it would be fine to donate a defibrillator but, under the circumstances, I would prefer that there was not to be a plaque bearing Cas's name beneath it.

I began to think there were just too many tributes being organised and this was hindering my ability to move forward away from the grief. I did appreciate the fact that Cas was so highly thought of – that was great – but it just became too much for me. I insisted that 'enough was enough' and that I didn't feel that I could carry their grief as well as my own. I realise now that was quite a harsh thing to have said.

–o0o–

'Positive thinking is a valuable tool that can help you overcome obstacles, deal with pain, and reach new goals'
Amy Morin

–o0o–

Looking back, did I ever feel guilty about some of those terrible thoughts I'd been experiencing, some of the things that I had said? Well, no, not at all. I feel my thoughts at that time were entirely justified.

When you go through such harsh grief *everything* is justified. You have just been through the most dreadful thing imaginable and, as far as you are concerned your grief is far worse than anybody else's. That's just how you feel at the time so there's no need to apologise for it.

Within a few months, however, I was feeling significantly better. I'd had a few consecutive good days, interspersed with many sad moments but these were overcome much more quickly than previously. I'd chatted with my boys about financial issues and arranged with them how I wanted to safeguard my assets.

I began to see more friends and, at last, began to feel more comfortable about being around couples. I was finding my running exercises were improving and I'd started a new gym regime and eating programme. I had also started to realise that I no longer wanted to invent a 'new me' but I would strive to find the 'old me' – the one that I actually liked!

Thank God, that sick feeling in the pit of my stomach had mostly subsided. I began to think more often about the boys and their loss and how they seemed to be coping so well. They were my strength and inspiration every single day. If they were okay, then I was okay.

(From my journal)

'A visit to the ATM has reduced me to tears. I went to use my cashpoint card. I quickly realised that I can use any account now. There are no separate accounts, they are all mine.'

Pete, the husband of Cas's late twin sister Chris, was also a great support. We couldn't have been more in a similar position. I saw him as a year ahead of me in the grief process. He seemed to be almost back on track which gave me hope each passing day. By now I was sleeping much better and no longer needing the herbal sleeping tablets I'd been taking since losing Cas.

Having got back to work, I began to feel much better overall. The weather was beginning to improve, the boys seemed to be doing well and, thanks to Pete's reassurance, I realised my progress was, on the whole, going quite well. In a better frame of mind I even began to think about making plans and having a holiday or weekend away.

Getting my health back proved to be the key to my recovery. I felt at peace knowing I had been a good wife, and I felt okay with everything we, as a family, had done since Cas died. We have respected his memory. This helped me draw a line under things. Most helpful though was talking to other widows and seeing at first hand how others have got through it.

Several months after Cas's death I travelled for a break in London with Ailsa who is a good friend from my schooldays. We saw the musical *Motown* and, afterwards, we popped into a wine bar. On leaving the bar we were passing an underground station where there was a busker. As he was playing he was trying to get passers-by up and dancing. Prior to losing Cas I had always been one of the first to get up onto a dance floor. Suddenly, Ailsa and I found ourselves dancing in the street.

–o0o–

'When life knocks you down, try to land on your back because, if you can look up, you can get up'

Les Brown

–o0o–

I felt I was back – what a brilliant feeling! With life getting busier I was beginning to feel more like the old me and that felt so good. A video of this was sent to the boys and I got a reply 'Mother is back!' It reinforced my knowledge that I was making progress.

One thing I knew for sure – I never, ever wanted a repeat of that dark pit of a hole I'd experienced over the past few months. That's not to say the tears had stopped flowing – I still had days when I needed a good cry, it's just that those days came less frequently than before. Certain memories would pop into my head and, that's it, I would be left feeling distraught again.

I would still get anxious about meeting friends who knew me and Cas as a couple. I felt far more comfortable seeing friends who were just 'my' friends.

And I still had moments of 'God, this is real' and dreaded some of the hurdles I would need to overcome in the future, such as graduations, weddings and so on.

I have since discovered a video on YouTube which, had I found it earlier, would have been a tremendous help. Entitled *The Train – an inspirational video*, to me, it seems to sum up perfectly the journey of our lives from birth to death. Follow this link to see for yourself:

https://youtube/AwFnQvFmvn4

It is what it is

IT IS almost inevitable that anyone would find their first year without a loved one the most difficult to cope with.

And, of course, the first birthday celebration or anniversary and Christmas can only serve to underline the loss you are feeling. But there are other occasions that have to be faced, such as the marriage of one of your children or the birth of a grandchild, in themselves, joyous occasions but, nevertheless, heartrending ones when you think of the joy your loved one is missing out on – the joy you so wish you could share with them – but I always remind myself that Cas doesn't know what he is missing, only I do.

This will, I'm afraid, be an ongoing situation. Unfortunately it's not a feeling you can totally eliminate but it is something you may be able to cope with in a more positive manner by looking at such events in a different way.

The anticipation, I believe, in the build-up to the occasion is usually worse than the actual day concerned. As a family we have now decided not to mark some occasions at all, mostly to spare us the pain of doing so but there are others who seem to think it is appropriate to remind us of the actual day that our lives changed forever. The cards kept coming on anniversaries, birthdays, date of death and date of funeral. Not once did a card arrive at any other time during the year, just to check in and ask you how things are!

Suddenly they are 'thinking of you'. Really, are they? Or are they satisfying their guilt of not having been in touch? I have since shared my thoughts and asked people not to send such reminders. We prefer to think that every experience coming up will be a new memory in Chapter Two of our lives.

The days leading up to my first Christmas without Cas saw my moods fluctuating wildly. Why does it have to be like this, I was thinking. Naturally, I couldn't get in the mood for Christmas but, with the family doing their best to make it as nice as possible for the grandchildren, I was becoming tired and anxious and finding it all rather too much to cope with. All I wanted was to be left alone and to be sad. Was that so wrong? I couldn't seem to get any joy from my grandchildren, my boys, friends or anything to do with Christmas.

To be fair, my boys were really good. Stephen, in particular, seemed to truly understand my mood swings and was aware of when I needed to be left alone for quieter moments. Sometimes I just wanted to scream out loudly: 'WHY ME AND WHY NOW!!'

A few weeks earlier I'd had the first of six counselling sessions with a psychotherapist. After most sessions I would feel much better. The counsellor was great. The first question I asked her was whether she was a widow. She replied that she was. That, to me, gave me the confidence in her ability to help me. She knew exactly how it felt to be in my situation. I can recall that every single time I visited her I would ask for reassurance that I would be alright.

We hit it off straight away. I really looked forward to our meetings. She joked that the first thing I always said to her was 'how are you?' and she would laugh and say, 'that's what I should be asking you!' Although the sessions cost £50 each, I really felt it was money well spent, such was the benefit I gained from them. It was me who called time on the sessions having had six of them.

The Christmas period proved challenging. On the 23rd we had a family dinner, 14 of us altogether which had been planned. The boys were great, Stephen had bought and cooked all the food but it was so hard to hold my head high, and so exhausting, especially when some people think it's okay to say 'Merry Christmas' to a recently bereaved person. Eventually, at around six o'clock, I took myself to my room for a rather large, noisy sob.

Christmas Eve was a better day. I had a 'lift me up' chat from James which really helped. I even managed a few smiles and, when playing some games, I even found myself laughing but, on Christmas Day itself, yet more 'Merry Christmas' messages were arriving on a day I was desperately hoping to treat as a

normal day. Merry Christmas – really? Did people really thing that I could be 'merry'? What would they like my reply to be?
In the morning Stephen returned to his home in Bath. I found his leaving to be hard to take as so many thoughts and memories had been running through my mind.
Mornings were definitely the toughest times of all for me at this stage. That's something that would need to change – and quickly. The early morning moods were dragging me into a pit before the day had even begun.
I couldn't wait to take the Christmas decorations down but, having guests meant I had to make an effort to be festive and cook when, really, I just wanted to stay in bed, not get dressed and just be left alone.
Knowing that James and Nura would soon be flying back to Denmark also made me so sad – another son going away – the prospect made me feel hollow and sick. I felt as if I was swimming against the tide. That night I wrote in my diary:

'Goodbye bloody Christmas 2018'.

Realising I needed to keep myself busy I decided to visit my brother Stephen who had been renting out an apartment in Spain. I flew out on Boxing Day. I booked a one-way ticket having decided to stay as long as it took to get my head together. In the back of my mind, I even thought about not coming back!
Stephen met me at the airport. And so began the start of even more extreme mood swings and contemplations about my future. I found myself getting angry that Stephen and Julie, my sister-in-law, were chatting as a couple and sharing morning cups of tea in bed. New Year's Eve turned out to be the most horrendous one I have ever experienced. I could hear everyone outside celebrating and fireworks going off. How can everyone else's life still be continuing? How can they be having fun when I am so distraught?
Julie did her best to reduce my anxieties. Every day she offered beauty therapy of one sort or another – nails, facials,

massage. I will be forever grateful for her attentive support, words of encouragement and listening to me constantly asking 'will I be okay?'

While in Spain I took up 'serious' running, managing to run 10k with little effort. Running made a huge difference to my well-being. My initial thoughts when in Spain were fleeting but nevertheless very worrying. I told no-one that I had considered 'slipping' off the cliff edge – it would appear to have been an accident.

Running changed those thought to ones of feeling that life could still be quite beautiful and worth living after all. I decided that I still had a lot to live for. I also realised that if I were to die Cas's death would have killed us both and that just wouldn't have been fair on our boys. I couldn't have done that to them, the grandchildren, my mum, family and friends. Maybe I'd been left behind for a reason. I just had to find that reason, my purpose.

I didn't stay long in Spain. I was thinking ahead. I decided to return home in time to meet my son James at Heathrow Airport as he was due home from Sri Lanka.

James had been so influential in trying to make me face life in the same way as Cas would have done and I wanted to be able to prove to him that I could not only drive to Heathrow on my own but be able to greet him on his arrival with a big hug and wearing a big welcoming smile on my face.

I had been a broken woman when he jetted off. It was important for me to prove to James that I had successfully begun to sort out the first of the three life boxes he had set before me. However, things didn't go quite as smoothly as I'd hoped. Driving to Heathrow I realised I'd become hopelessly lost and it was only after I phoned my brother-in-law Pete for directions that I found the right road.

Although the journey had been stressful, it had been worth it. James later told me that, as soon as he saw me waiting for him, arms open and smiling, he believed it had been a defining moment and that, in time, I would be okay.

Buoyed by making it to and from Heathrow, the next day I was feeling pretty good. The past few days had gone well and for the final time, I saw my therapist which was a very good feeling.
Cas had always been so pragmatic and positive; he was a realist. His interest in other cultures and mysticism was highlighted after his death when we were looking through his book collection. He had highlighted several passages in them that had particularly caught his attention.
Slowly but surely I found myself believing some of Cas's points of view, phases that he believed to be true. Phases that had previously been so alien and annoying to me, were now making perfect sense.
Whatever will be, will be – It is what it is.

–o0o–

'If you can't fly then run, if you can't run then walk, if you can't walk then crawl, but whatever you do you have to keep moving forward'
                         Martin Luther King Jr

–o0o–

Fighting back

SOONER or later, following a bereavement, you will need to return to some form of normality in your life. This is never going to be easy. After such a devastating event has disrupted your life and dreams, you owe it to yourself to regain some form of structure in order to begin the next phase of your life.
Obviously, it is best to do this in a sensible and well thought-out manner – and definitely not in the way that I did! By making snap decisions and, by acting impulsively, I could have found out the hard way that this was not the best way forward – as you will soon read.
So, on reflection, I would strongly advise anyone not to rush in to any major decisions, to consult with trusted family members or friends before doing anything rash because, if you don't, you could well regret it later.
Try to revisit your hobbies as much as you can. If the memories are too harsh – for instance, if a hobby was one you partook with your loved one, maybe that might prove too difficult to return to. If this is the case, try to find a new interest, something that could mark a new chapter in your life. It's time to make new memories. Is there anything you have always fancied trying? This could be the time.
Of course, we all react differently to grief. In my case it was quite extreme as you have read. All sorts of thoughts need to be processed after your world has been shaken to its core and there are no right or wrong ways to express them. It is, after all, grief.
People should not be judged by their reactions to a sudden and life-changing event such as the death of a much loved partner. And, of course, while some may consider their own lives to be over, others, particularly those not yet in the more advanced stages of life, may feel they have a lot more living to do.
I set myself some challenges. I was determined to prove that, without Cas, I could manage on my own. That was not a bad aspiration, it's just that I was far too impulsive. Had it not

been for my boys and one or two other people with my best interests at heart, I could have ended up in a terrible situation.
I wanted to prove to my boys that I could look after myself. I needed to take the pressure off them from looking after me and giving them the time that they needed to grieve for their father and to get on with their own lives.
I remember writing in my journal . . .

'Hate these really flat days – too much hanging around in the mornings. Need to be busy, busy, busy.'
'I want stability, in the form of a constant feeling that I will be ok.
'I want the boys to see that I'm ok.
'I will go to New York.
'I want a life companion to share my next chapter with, to take care of me so that the boys don't have to.
'I believe, and I want it to be with someone that I know, that the family knows. Someone who will love me.
'I want it to be different and understand that I can't compare.
'I want a step grandad for Jack and Harrison and future generations. I don't know if they will call him 'grandad' or if I would want them to?
'I want my mum to see me happy again.
'I want these things by next Christmas so that I can enjoy the festivities like any other family.
'I want to be able to see fathers with their sons without feeling the gut -wrenching pain that I currently endure.
'I want to watch the rugby without painful memories.
'I want to write and publish a book about this unwanted journey. I want it to help others on their journey.
'I feel positive that I will have all of these things – because I deserve to.'

I was gradually getting my life back into some form of order. Another widow, Betty, was really struggling. One day I took her shopping. She was feeling so lonely. This resulted in me feeling really low myself. I realised that at this stage of my

journey, it was too hard to support others. However, very soon that changed.
When I got home a wave of anxiety and hollowness flooded over me and I had a good cry for 10 minutes. I was so exhausted afterwards. For a while I felt like a zombie then, afterwards, I was okay.
However, buoyed by my successful trips to airports and flights abroad, I threw myself into a number of projects. I felt an overwhelming need to show everyone that I had emerged from the fog that I had been in. I wanted people to see me as a person getting on with my life, someone who was getting things done.
Having been a dog owner, I decided I would volunteer to support the Cinnamon Trust which is a country-wide charity that cares for pets. If their owners pass on or end up in nursing homes, their pets are cared for by volunteers. I just needed to feel useful and for people to see me as someone who was getting things done, for my sons to see I was moving forward with my life.
But there was still more to do if I was to be able to say I had completed the first of the life box targets James had set me. Meeting other widowed friends eventually did help me get over the initial feelings of deep grief. I began to realise that, despite my down days, mentally, I was already in a better state than some of them.
I've always liked to be the go-to person when people are struggling. I have always been a caring person – that's why I went into nursing. I found that some within the group were really struggling. I was able to comfort them on the occasional days I was feeling stronger. They would then do the same for me on their good days.
Every time I achieved something I considered significant, I felt uplifted. I would Whatsapp the boys so they could see that I wasn't just sitting at home crying. I believed if they could see that, they could be getting on with their own lives instead of worrying about me.

Looking back I guess it was a kind of 'Look at me, I'm looking after dogs; look at me, I'm helping other widows; look at me, I'm helping the elderly – look at how well I've done!' For a while, that was my driving force. I guess I wanted people to look at me and see a survivor.

–o0o–

'In the process of letting go you will lose many things from the past, but you will find yourself'
Depak Chopra

–o0o–

For me it was about going back to proving I could do it. It was about ticking boxes, making myself do things even though I didn't really feel like it. I had to make the effort whilst still acknowledging I needed to grieve. I set up a white board to tick off my daily achievements, another idea from James.

Not everything I planned worked out so well. I felt I had to prove to the world I was the person 'saving others'. After all, I had set up a bereavement group and was actively helping others. I wanted to help people on a practical level but I soon realised I couldn't do that in the way I'd hoped. The training to be a bereavement counsellor did not work out.

Sometimes I would still curl up into a ball and cry but I made myself get up, get showered and get on with something. That could be to make a list of things to do, maybe go for a walk, or do some shopping. I made 30 individual shepherd's pie meals, vegetables included. This was to ensure that I would be able to have a decent meal every day for a month with very little effort.

I realised I had to MAKE myself do things, the alternative would have been to get into a rut that would have been very difficult to get out of.

There were so many ideas racing around in my head as I tried to make plans for the future. I was going to get dogs. I was going to work for Age Concern so I could befriend the elderly. I even applied for a nursing job in Hertfordshire and another job to work with elephants. I thought I might take a world cruise or sell my house. Or I would take off so no-one could find me. Even now, I still have thoughts of disappearing!

As you can see, my mind was all over the place. So much so that within a short time of losing Cas I could no longer face living my life for the next 25 to 30 years without a companion by my side. I tried joining all sorts of groups – a rambling club was one of the first groups I joined in the hope of meeting a companion – I didn't care too much at the time what sort of person he might be – I just wanted a significant other in my life.

I looked at almost every man that passed me to see if he had a wedding ring on his finger. I was willing to have any man alive with me just so long as I wasn't on my own. I felt desperate to be needed, wanted and loved.

Thoughts turned to our Clacton male friends. Some had already made 'friendship suggestions'. At first the attention seemed that it could be worth considering. But it's worth remembering that I was willing to consider anyone as a companion. These were not thoughts from someone of a sound mind but of someone who was confused, lonely, desperate and in the depths of raw grief. My thoughts now: Ridiculous, madness, and how dare they?

At the time I just did not realise how vulnerable I was. Or perhaps I just wasn't in the right frame of mind to accept that fact. So many people warned me against making any rash decisions but I just stared at them and told them I would do what I wanted. 'This is my life, I'm on my own. I can do what I want!'

When I wanted to sell my home I was warned it was not a good idea, but I didn't want to hear that. Looking back though, I'm so glad I didn't go through with it and that I eventually came to my senses. Fortunately, my family and close friends formed a tight pack around me, watching every move I made. Whatever would have happened if not for them? They protected me from myself.

I began to avoid going to familiar supermarkets. I was so worried about bumping into people that we had both known. I knew that once again, those pitying looks would be offered along with the empty platitudes.

Working at the nursing home continued and I was back in the gym. However, these routines were a constant reminder of life as it once was. Both doing our own thing then coming together at the gym. On the drive home from the gym it reminded me of the times Cas and I would work out and compare our fitness figures. He'd ask how far I'd run on the treadmill and how many calories I burned.

One of my friends, Harry, was always so grateful whenever I visited him. He loved the company. He'd lost his wife so we often chatted together. He used to tell me how much my visits helped him. What Harry didn't realise was how much our chats helped ME as I'd called in on him on my way home from the gym. This always diverted any unwanted memories.

Quite often, having been to the gym, I would get home, have a shower, curl up in bed and the tears would flow. After a while, I began to realise I could pull myself out of it. I could think positive thoughts. I started visiting other friends after the gym, getting home late and exhausted enough to quickly fall asleep.

Thank you to my friend Caroline who encouraged me to pop in whenever I wanted to – I did often! Thank you also for sending me three kisses (XXX) every day for a year. No other comments were needed.

My friend Yanna would drop everything to pop over to mine or I would pop into hers. She often arrived with her two dogs and we would light the fire, watch TV. Only when I started to nod off, would she go home. I am so grateful to have these two exceptional friends in my life – friends that ask no questions and expect no words.

I quickly regained my fitness and my weight improved too. Physically, I was feeling much better. I was happier in the gym and stopped putting off returning home.

It was when the boys were sorting through the office that a Windsor half marathon certificate was found. When Cas was young he had entered the half marathon and had completed the course in the not too shabby time of 93 minutes so the gauntlet had been laid. And so it was that the boys and my sister Jeanette and I entered the Windsor half marathon.

The boys did really well – not beating their father's time – but completing the course in a very good time of 103 minutes. As for myself and my sister, we completed the 13.1 miles in just over three hours. We had ended the event limping around the course, and my hips were in agony!

The half marathon had been one of four goals I had set myself, the remaining three being to take some of Cas's ashes to India – a place he had always wanted to visit; to get a plaque sorted out and, finally, to jump out of an aeroplane.

It's good to talk

IT IS hard to under-estimate the importance of talking to each other about your wishes in the event of your death. Fortunately, this was a topic Cas and I raised on several occasions and this proved to be such a relief when the time came to sort out his funeral as I knew exactly what his wishes were. Sadly though, his wishes to be an organ donor were not able to be honoured.

There is so much to sort out following a death, much of which can be done fairly straight-forwardly, particularly if you are fortunate enough to have the help and support of family members.

But, inevitably, some companies and organisations prove far trickier to deal with than others while some, it appears, seem to do their utmost to make any dealings with them as difficult as possible.

Hopefully, by reading some of my experiences I can offer you some pointers to make you aware of what could help you through a minefield of bureaucracy that you may be dealing with now.

Cas and I were always organised and we believed we had adequately prepared for the event of one of our deaths. Among the first things I had to deal with was the funeral. Because of our chats, I knew exactly what Cas would have wanted.

I knew he wanted to be cremated, I knew what sort of service he would have wanted, what clothes to wear, what music he would have wanted, and the eulogy almost wrote itself, such was the depth we had broached the subject in the past. Had we not had those chats, organising Cas's funeral would have been so much harder.

We had also discussed and made our wills – another vitally important thing to do because, without a will, a deceased person's estate would be declared intestate – this means their estate/property would have to be shared out according to the rules of intestacy.

If a will has been made it is important to have been made out in the correct manner. In the event of the will being declared invalid, it is not the wishes of the deceased that are carried out as the rules of intestacy will take precedence. Ensure that bank accounts, passwords and wishes are discussed with your family.

However, as prepared as we thought we were, I faced many hurdles. Cas had several accounts, policies and contracts that had been taken out in his name only and it took me more than a year to sort everything out and to transfer these into my name.

Computer passwords – that's another really important thing. You should always let a 'trusted other' know the passwords to any laptops, computers, mobile phones. Here's a good example – the Dartcharge, the online payment scheme for motorists crossing the Queen Elizabeth Bridge between Essex and Kent. Our account had been set up in Cas's name which meant I could not set up another account with the same address. I could not remove his car from the account or put my car on the account because I had no log on details.

I could not access a mobile phone bank account as I had no PIN. Cas leased a BMW in his own name but, even though he died, that did not release me from the contract. The lease company made me buy the car off them for £38,000 and then I had to sell it to recoup the money. The contract had stated these terms in very small writing

To help your family in the future I would recommend getting an *Advanced Planning of Care* book from any hospice – it's a large booklet with so much useful information in it and there's also a service called *Tell Us Once* which is really useful. You can telephone them and give a National Insurance number. Details of this service is in the *Useful Information* section at the end of this story. Furnished with your information they can close down bank accounts, change names on things, take a name off council tax and polling lists. However, ensure that family empty bank accounts if they can before contacting them. As soon as the banks are phoned, the relevant bank accounts are shut down preventing any access.

Another problem I encountered concerned the solar panels which had been installed on our roof which were not in my name. It took me a year of telephone calls, emails and letters to get that contract switched over into my name. At first the company refused to even discuss the problem with me because the contract had not been in my name.

In the meantime, the build up of credit generated from the panels was going into an account I had no access to. I had to continually badger the bereavement team at EON to sort things out.

I would also advise you to look into the prospect of taking out Lasting Power of Attorneys (LPoAs) naming a family member as executor for both Health & Welfare and Finances. With these it is possible for family members or friends to take over responsibility for you in regards to care and all financial aspects without battling with banks etc in order to do so.

However, this is something you need to do whilst you are of sound mind. In other words, the benefactor has full mental capacity when giving his or her permission for a nominated person to take over affairs. The power of attorney is only activated if mental capacity is deemed to be absent.

Sometimes this can prove to be very expensive. However, it can be done free of charge and without the need to pay for the services of a solicitor, For instance, if the person you intend to represent is in receipt of Pension Credit, the charge may be waived entirely if the LPoAs are applied for online. Fortunately, this is not a particularly complicated procedure.

At the moment, I consider myself to have full mental capacity which is why, in the light of what has happened regarding Cas, I intend to take out LPoAs so that my boys do not have to worry about such things in the event that I ever become unable to take care of my own affairs.

I will also be arranging my own complete funeral package and I will ensure that everything I can think of is put down in writing to make everything as straight forward as possible for the boys. Wishes that can be activated when I am either unable to handle my own affairs or after I have passed on. Assets have been transferred into a property company as a tribute to Cas. Morehen Company Ltd is growing as the years go by – all credit to the boys. This has been done now so that I can see the boys benefit from one half of their inheritance.

It's amazing how many companies insist that you provide a death certificate to prove that a policy account holder has died. It's worth letting executors know to get at least 10 copies printed. Also to be prepared for many trips to the post office. Most documentation necessary will need to be sent by recorded delivery.

There are some ways, however, of saving money, not all of which are widely publicised. It is possible to apply for a single person's council tax and there is also a widow's pay-out, known as a Bereavement Payment, which pays out £2,000 straight away from the Department of Work and Pensions, and then £100 a month for a year (Search online at *Bereavement Payment – GOV.UK* for details).

You can also cut down on your utility bills. Several online bereavement forums offer really useful information in this respect. They have expert advisors who can help you save quite a bit of cash.

It's worth looking at your current media package. For example will you now need the whole package, such as the sports channel? You will find that the monthly costs can be significantly reduced.

Introducing Plan B

I AM 100 percent sure that Cas would have wanted the boys and I to live our lives. I know he would have hated the thought of me being curled up in a ball, crying and in despair.

If he could look down on me and see that, I know he would be heartbroken. I am sure that he would be so pleased that we, as a family, are moving forward in a positive manner and supporting his memory in so many ways.

He would want us to believe that he is still with us. That he remains with us in the form of energy because, as I have already stated, he firmly believed that energy lives on and is all around us.

I now believe this to be the case. I became sure that, if he could tell us he was still around, he would. There have been several odd occurrences that lead me to believe that he is still with us (as stated in my journal).

Early in 2018, Cas and I decided to take up musical instruments. I began to learn to play the ukulele and he began to learn to play a tin whistle. We had joked that we would like to perform a surprise 'family concert' on my 60th birthday.

To be honest, I was useless on the ukulele, surpassed only by Cas's uselessness with the tin whistle! He only ever learnt two notes. However, since he died, I have frequently heard those two notes. This was recorded in my journal and mentioned in the earlier part of this book.

In the first two months after Cas died, whenever I heard those notes they were very loud then, over the next few months, they seemed to fade – could that have been the time he went from nowhere to wherever he is now? – and, since then, the notes have come back to me time and again.

I know some readers will think this is rubbish. I don't blame them. I don't believe in any of that sort of thing normally, but I really do believe this is Cas's way of letting me know he is still around and looking over me.

One of Cas's favourite songs was *Come on Eileen* by Dexy's Midnight Runners. The boys and I always teased him about his choice because he could never dance to it. It seemed to come on the radio all the time. As did songs by David Bowie, another favourite. Nonsense maybe, but the boys are convinced their dad is close to them, as I believe he is close to me.

This belief pushes us along on this journey. We strive to 'show' Cas that we can 'do this' We will make him proud, content; so that he can sleep easy.

–o0o–

'We must let go of the life we have planned, so as to accept the one that is waiting for us'
Joseph Campbell

–o0o–

After a bereavement you need to consider close family and friends. As I've already mentioned, I don't like the term 'moving on'. I prefer 'moving forward'. That could mean anything, not necessarily a new relationship.

My first priority has, and always will be, my boys. Their feelings are paramount for me. I know that they would want me to be happy. If someone, or *something* makes you happy, then go with it whilst being sensitive to other's feelings.

The third life box set out for me by James was the box dealing with heartbreak and loneliness. In the summer of 2019 I was beginning to feel that I had physically and emotionally improved. I was beginning to cope a little better with my new situation.

Life with Cas had always been my Plan A but that had been cruelly snatched away from me and I realised that, if life was to go on for me, I would have to settle for a Plan B. This plan could never be as good as Plan A but I owed it to myself and my family to make Plan B as good as I possibly could.

For me though, the third box would only be filled if I could, one day, meet someone. I know to some bereaved people that would not be a consideration but I felt I really needed someone to share my life with.

I will never have children with another partner. It is unlikely that I will be making decisions regarding house buying and setting up a home. I have my home. I will, however, be able to embrace fun, adventures and new possibilities without the stresses that youth bring. It is possible that I can find love again, be loved again but not be truly 'in love.' I accept this completely because I don't want it. I've experienced my one and only true love.

Some people, after a bereavement, want to meet someone almost straight away, like I did – but, on reflection, I know that this was to fill the void, to be part of a couple, to ease the loneliness at that time. Some people insist they will NEVER meet anyone else in the belief that to do so would be a betrayal to their loved one; some people believe they could only ever love one person, while others just bide their time until they can be reunited with their loved one, but how long should you leave it before looking for companionship?

Well, there are no rules and everyone is different.

–o0o–

'Holding on is believing that there is only a past; Letting go is knowing that there's a future'
Daphne Rose Kingma

–o0o–

Pete, (my brother-in-law) Chris, Cas and I had always been on good terms, after all, we were family.

By now Pete was in his second year without Chris. Following her death, Cas and I had offered him support. Following Cas's death, Pete had done likewise for me and, on occasions, we'd had lunch together and chatted for hours.

There is so much shared history between us, so many people we both know. My boys and Chris's girls are cousins, so there have been many family events that we both have attended. I also know Pete's girls well as they lived with Pete and Chris and her girls for many years.

Being in each other's company is easy. Talking about our loss is easy as we understand each other's emotions. Reminiscing about them is easy. It comes easy to offer support when it is needed. I cook for Pete, he puts up the shelves!

A routine began. One week I would go to Pete's for lunch, the next week he would come to my house. For both of us it was nice to have the companionship again. Going to the cinema with someone felt good.

Pete and I realise that fate has played a massive part in our union. We are aware that without our losses, our union would never have happened. At our ages we have minimal stress, no youngsters to constantly consider. Neither of us have 'baggage' and both are independently self sufficient.

For us, it's all about having fun and going places in the motor home that I purchased at the end of 2019. We intend to make new memories and just continue to settle into our new normal. We both continue to be sensitive to feelings and emotions from both sides of our families and would never intentionally upset any of them.

We continue to be respectful to our lost loved ones and will forever take them with us on our journey. My boys remain supportive of every decision that I have made and are happy that I am happy.

Pete's girls have also embraced the new situation and are also happy because Pete is happy. Chris's girls are also very happy. As for anyone else, I have no desire to worry about their thoughts or, indeed, seek any approval.

As a family, we have done our very best to respect Cas's memory and we will continue to do so. I decided to have my wedding ring and engagement rings melted down and remoulded into a single ring; we organised a rugby match, sponsored a rugby club and a music festival for the past two years and had his name emblazoned on the back of sports shirts; and set up a MCL Ltd in his honour. We have run the half marathon; got tattoos and I have written this book.

We honour his life every day by following in his footsteps. Footsteps that lead to a life of achieving and living the best life that we can. And I mean really living, not just surviving!

Now I have to do my best to ensure Plan B – my life from now on – is going to be as good as I can possibly make it. Cas will *never* be forgotten and he will *always* be in my heart but life has to go on. I owe it to myself and my family and just keep telling myself 'Que sera sera, it is what it is.'

–oOo–

'Letting go doesn't mean that you don't care about someone any more. It's just realising the only person you have control over is yourself'
Deborah Reber

–oOo–

Rotary Club President: Cas proudly wears his chain of office.

Happy family: Cas and I pose for a photo with our sons James, Daniel and Stephen.

Apples of our eyes: Cas and Daniel with our grandchildren Harrison and Jack.

Little treasures: Grandsons Harrison and Jack.

Cycling fanatic: Cas was rarely happier than when he was in the saddle.

In his element: Cas was fascinated by Chinese and Indian cultures.

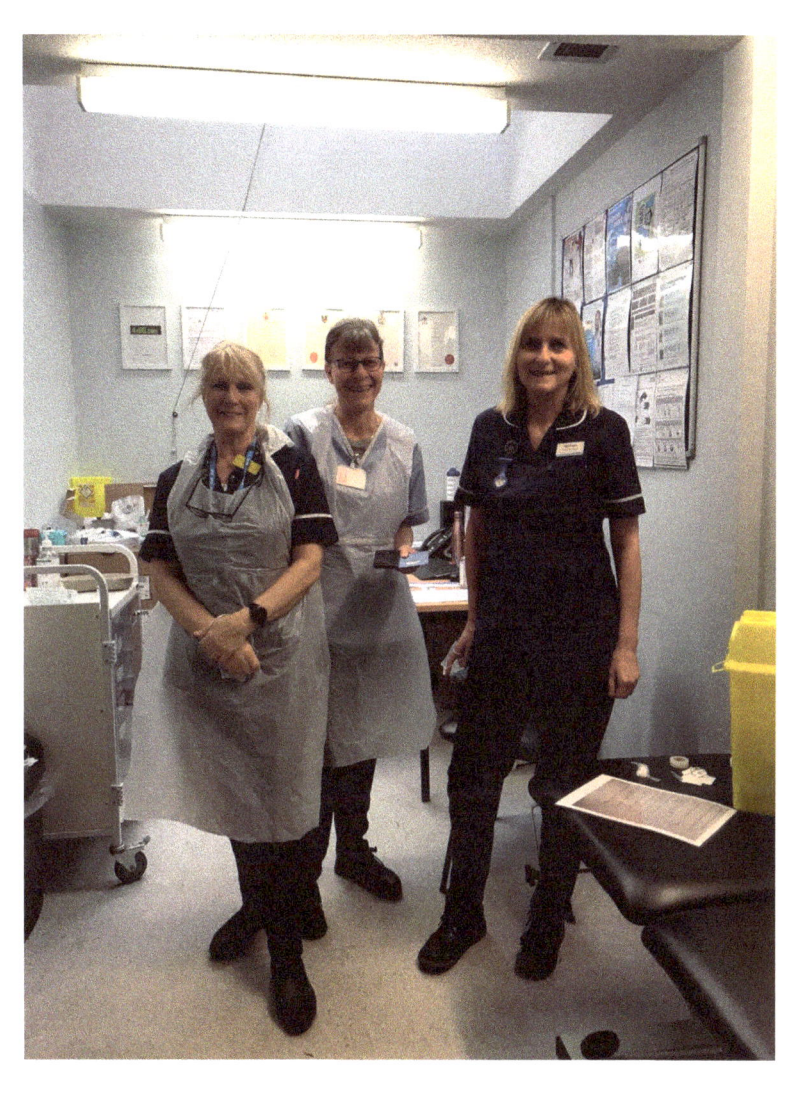

Cousins reunited: This picture was taken on January 17th, 2020 when I met up with my cousins Alison and Gill (centre and right) to administer Covid 19 vaccinations at the same clinic.

Our tributes; our way of honouring Cas's memory

Here I am with my sister Jeanette (left) having completed a 10km run in preparation for the Windsor half marathon.

We did it! The Windsor half marathon ticked and completed.

So proud of these three.

My forever ring: both wedding rings, my eternity and engagement ring were melted down and remodelled.

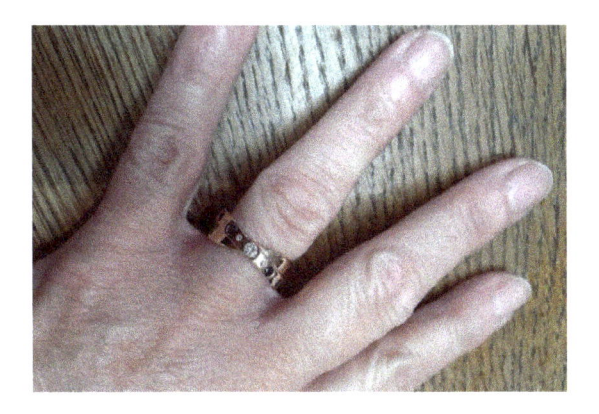

A thing of the past – a spiral of despair.

A poignant reminder – a train passenger wearing a a hat with a Wasps logo.

Another possibility? Keeping the family name alive. This remains 'just an idea'.

I made it!

Fourteen months later

I decided I would like to summarise the first year. A year that I was told would be the worst – it was!
This idea had been at the forefront of my mind for a while so I felt compelled to begin. I wrote the following without referring to the notes and journal I had kept, but the events and emotions flooded back to me as clear as though they happened yesterday.

There were only a few words written initially – *HELL, DEVASTATION, PANIC etc.*

As the days and weeks progressed, I lent into the raw grief, realising that there was nothing else I could do. I had people buzzing around offering all sorts of support but there was nothing anyone could do to ease the pain. My thoughts were all over the place and, at times, very dark. The dark veil continued to engulf me without warning.
As a nurse I knew that my physical well-being was paramount. I had lost a lot of weight during the first week. Hyper-ventilating, palpitations and sheer panic dominated my day – most of the day.
Along with help from my son James, we researched the best 'widow' books to read. I am not keen on reading, but I stuck to those six books like glue. I started eating heaps of protein, made a month's worth of shepherd's pie which I ate every day and got back to the gym quickly.
For me, I needed to know that I would be okay both physically and emotionally. I needed positive reading and positive people around me. This is when I became selective about who I would be around. I found comfort amongst other widows who were further on in their journey and who had not only survived

but were living. I eventually felt good about supporting others, it was cathartic.

I travelled extensively, including an amazing visit to New York – just to prove to myself that I could. I wanted the boys to feel proud of me. I ensured that I was busy on all of the 'firsts.' I came to realise that for me there were two key strategies that I would be using to get me through:
1. To almost hibernate from the reality, from well-meaning people who showered me with pity.
2. To understand that I was not someone who wanted to live a single life, although very independent, I had too much to give to another – maybe for another 30 years! That's a long time to be on your own and there was no way I wanted that.

The hibernation worked.

I re-emerged as a stronger individual who had been spared from well-meaning people with their empty platitudes and trite comments. I came to realise that I still had so much in my life worth being here for.

Those that know me understood that I didn't want, or indeed, need pity. That understanding included knowing how long to leave me alone before attempting to get in touch again. Those that didn't understand are no longer my friends.

My frantic decision making has calmed down and I have a clear picture of where I want to be and who I want to be. In fact, I want the 'old me' back. I no longer want to reinvent myself.

My character is returning – my sense of fun is back. Pete and I are enjoying time together, planning and having fun. He is someone that we all know and trust.

We are a couple, a partnership. We are embracing this new life, albeit unplanned. I am no longer half a couple but part of a whole one and it's a great, reassuring feeling. My mum is now happy that I am happy. I remain cautious and sensitive to all those that matter.

The initial thoughts of 'why me?' 'why him?' 'it's unfair' have subsided and I now think 'why not me?' 'what makes me exempt? The harsh reality is that death comes to us all, we will all lose a partner. When is the right time? After 30 plus years together or 64 years?
When I sit and reflect, my conclusion is that I can have a Chapter Two, another stab at this life; I have time!

–o0o–

'To be strong is to reach out your hand and grab hold of the future. Not a future of despair from the past, but a future that is what you make it, a future filled with hope for, without love, we may never attain a purpose'
Andrew Lopes

–o0o–

Cas played his last card exactly how he wanted – not to suffer. Yes, I would have loved the boys to have had their father in their lives for longer. However, they have a whole life of plans. They all have partners and are happy. They accepted that at some point they would lose a parent. They say it was the right order of the circle of life.
As a family we understood that their healing is my healing and vice versa. I see very clearly that they are healing, their lives are continuing. I think that they see the same for me.
I strive forward, continually trying to achieve, make the boys proud and above all reassure them that I am okay. We are all in touch daily with photos, silly jokes and videos. My grandsons, Jack and Harrison, are in my thoughts daily and I see them more regularly. They like Pete and he is an enormous help when I have them. They don't call him grandad.

I will continue to live quietly unnoticed, for now anyway! There will be no Facebook pictures or comments relating to sombre dates. Neither will there be information regarding my life choices. People are very quick to judge. There will be no attendance at events with the Rotarians and my 'couple' Clacton friends – not yet. I shall choose carefully what to attend, when and who with.

So how am I now? There have been many ups and downs. As a family we have remembered a wonderful man who lived a life of pursuing his goals. He lived life to the full with positivity and integrity. It was with him in everything he did. We have remembered his way of living and will live our lives by the same standards.

I wanted the first year to be about honouring his ethos of life, at the same time wishing the year away as quickly as possible. I have done everything possible to find 'me' again, which I have.

I have almost closed the lid on the three boxes in my efforts to recover. I have managed to crawl my way out of the dark, dark hole (the spiral charity box). There have been minimal emotions that have led me to fall back in. People's well-meaning comments no longer make me as angry. I am almost accepting of everyone's right to live.

I still cannot accept the lottery of life, how it is decided that some die whilst others live. The feelings of our family and indeed the community being cheated remain. To lose someone that had so much to give to us and many others is a huge loss. I still think that it is so unfair that those that have little to offer, albeit because of choice or circumstances are living – sorry but that's how I feel, That feeling has not subsided and I don't think that it ever will.

I do feel disappointed with some people. People that I felt should have been more supportive. Those that made empty promises, who declared they would stay in touch. The very people who know me well enough to attempt to make contact again and would know I would have responded. It's a much easier option to not make contact than feeling awkward when they do. The damage is done and some of these relationships may never fully recover.

I never went to India, worked with elephants, or moved to Hertfordshire. I decided against working on a cruise ship and setting up the 'healing on wheels' service. I also didn't become a counsellor. I am still considering if I will start up a garden business next year.

I didn't jump out of a plane, but did experience the largest zip wire ride in the UK. I never did invite 'just anyone' to move in. My return to Denmark to meet Orjan in the café did not happen. I never disappeared. I did enjoy the Christmas of 2019. We all went skiing.

I can now watch the rugby and see fathers with their sons, although it makes me sad. I am accepting that I've been blessed with the building of my nest, raising a family and encouraging them to fly. Others are entitled to do this – It's their turn.

AND, YES I HAVE WRITTEN A BOOK – THIS ONE!

I am now certain that I will stay in this house, our family home, that I will live a full, active and happy life.

I will strive to be the best matriarch that a family can have. One that is supportive of all those that I love and cherish. One that accepts that I can't have my old life back but understand that I can have an alternative, different life – an Option B.

'A life changing event, doesn't have to be a life ending one.'

I think of Cas every day and wonder where he is and I am sure that he can make contact. He does this through the poignant songs that come onto the radio at key points of the day, the fading sound of the tin whistle and the robin that perches by my side when I'm in the garden.

**'Those that we love don't go away
They walk beside us every day
Unseen, Unheard, but always near
So loved, so missed, so dear'**

(words written on a robin sculpture)

June 2019 (from my journal)

'Wow, I was dreading James' 30th birthday event. Went better than expected. No meltdowns – might have been the drink! Another thing ticked off. Vintage tea hosted here for the Rotarians. Proved to be a very long emotional day. Maybe this was due to the average age of 75 plus and varying disabilities. The disturbing thoughts resurfaced 'how can all these people still be here?'
'Just the graduation to get through – a tough event that will be.'

July 2019 (from my journal) My last entry:

'Hello journal, it's been 4 weeks since I have written anything. Here is an update about how I feel these days . . .
'Graduation went better than I thought it would. We all supported each other. Another milestone ticked off. I return to the memories of those days when we used to remark on how happy and lucky we were to have such a happy life. It wasn't just said now and then, but most days as we enjoyed our everyday existence.
'I still cannot believe that the bubble just burst and in an instant that life was gone. I have a constant reminder of the unit that has been shattered. That one cog on the wheel is missing. When I see the boys, it pulls at my heart strings that they have no father. Jack and Harrison have no grandad. Today there were tears, but not for long. They are never far away but don't flow as often and as harsh as they did.
'The boys are buzzing about the property company – MCL. It's good to see, but bloody hell, it's come about at a huge cost. Their excitement, my loss, albeit we had no choice.
'I feel cheated and denied what should have been. I feel isolated from the 'couple' friends that I have shared 30 years with, have memories with. But how can I reunite with them as a single person? I don't want to.

'Sometimes I don't want to be the head of the family, the nannie. It feels like a burden to appear okay, to put on a front. I feel frantic most of the time, planning and goal setting. I am so very tired.
'This week, I feel totally lost in my direction. I have lost all purpose. I desperately need a purpose, to feel useful.
'I know tomorrow, I will feel different.'
August 2019 onwards saw a gradual, positive recovery.

Conclusion
2021

A lot has changed, I've changed mentally and physically. I have a new hip, a new drive to regain a better fitness. I have my motor home, my trips. My garden is constantly evolving with new ideas. I now have planning back in my life.

My purpose in life, a purpose that I was so desperate to find, was sent to me in late 2020. Covid 19 had struck, the pandemic began to take control. I was asked to assist with the fight against it. I have been vaccinating for 10 months now and been involved in the preparation and giving of over 8,000 vaccinations. My purpose continues . . .
The subsequent lockdown worked in my favour in so many ways. I was able to resume my hibernation from society as there was no choice. I was not seen as being insular, just doing as I was told. We were only allowed to mix within our bubble after all! I enjoyed extra time with Stephen whilst he spent the year at home.
Pete and I spent time apart, time to think about future plans. We were able to consider if our union was a desperate 'need' to be part of a couple. Or had we grown together for us to 'Want' to be part of a couple? Need and want are very different concepts.
My life continues, Pete's life continues. We constantly chat about our losses and feel grateful that we can support each other in a way that no-one else could. We have shared history between both our families. It is a situation that was presented to us following surprising and tragic circumstances. We know we are Options B and Pete understands when I say to him that I am 'on loan' for 25 plus years, we hope.
We plan a united journey of fun and adventures but when my time comes, I will return to my Option A. My funeral is arranged, The Power of Attorneys are sorted, I have a revised

will. My final resting place is secured at Old Park Meadow, next to the legend that is Cas. I will reunite with him and rest in peace amongst the wild flowers, and the beautiful, peaceful backdrop of the rural countryside.

I think about how I have come back to being 'me'. How life challenges have given me an inner strength so powerful that I have been able to dig deep, use the strength and recover.

When I say 'recover', I am referring to a recovery from feeling as though I would forever be in that dark pit of that spiral charity pot. A release from that dark grey veil that was forever lurking around me. To recover enough to banish all thoughts of disappearing, of having an 'accident'.

Enough recovery that gives me the pure pleasure of sound sleep and a healthy appetite. Such is this recovery that I can now see and enjoy the simple pleasures of life – the birds singing, the change of the seasons. The profound joy of seeing and hearing the grandchildren laugh. The admiration for the unity that the boys show both socially and with business.

I can see and appreciate what others have done for me and continue to do. I can also understand how my aggressiveness towards others could have been perceived as hurtful and unkind.

Life goes on, the wheels are still spinning, the world is still turning. I understand and accept all of this – death is part of the circle of life, as is birth. These are definite events that we can be sure of.

I continue to vaccinate and accept the different world that I currently live in. The larger world that has been thrown into chaos and my own world, where I navigate my way through Option B.

I often think about what I have, what is ahead, and I feel grateful.

Concluded November 2021. (Printed in 2022 due to Covid delays.)

–o0o–

The following words have been of great comfort to me. Hopefully, they will be just as comforting for you too:

*You can shed tears because they are gone,
or you can smile because they lived.*

*You can close your eyes and pray they will come back,
or you can open your eyes and see all they left for you.*

*Your heart can be empty because you can't see them,
or you can be full of the love you shared.*

*You can turn your back on tomorrow and live yesterday,
or you can be happy for tomorrow because of yesterday.*

*You can remember only that they are gone,
or you can cherish their memory and let it live on.*

*You can cry and close your mind and feel empty,
or you can do what they would want . . .*

*Smile, Open your heart, Love . . .
and go on.*

Elizabeth Ammons
lessonslearnedinlife.com

Acknowledgements

First and foremost, I give my heartfelt thanks to my three boys: Daniel, James and Stephen. They were and continue to be here for me. Without them, I am not sure that I would be here. My desire to now be here for them overrides any negative thoughts that I still, very occasionally, get. Thank you for listening to my random, frantic plans and allowing me to arrive at my own conclusions regarding them. Huge respect to you all for supporting every decision that I have made on this unplanned journey.

Thank you also to Carrie, Nura and Alex for looking after my boys. Carrie, your encouragement to do 'whatever I want' was my starting point to where I am now.

Pete, thank you for your continued support. The kind of support that no-one else could offer. Support from you is from someone who really knows and understands the highs and lows. Thank you for our plans, adventures and more plans! Sincere thanks for just being you. And well done for coping so well with the challenges that I present.

My dear friends Yanna and Caroline. True friends that were 'just there'. No fuss offered as they knew I didn't want it.

Thank you also to Libby for acknowledging my requests when I returned to The Manor.

Thank you Tom and Lou for checking that I was okay.

Thank you Alisa for taking me to New York and introducing me to Gin, of every flavour!

My gym and spin buddies for your encouragement and inclusion – thank you. Sue, I've enjoyed our walks.

Dear Jeanette, little sis. It was hard for you, but you showed me how to continue. You are a special 'Bennetty Boo' little sis! I think that you knew that *I* would 'come back!'

Mum, it was also hard for you. In your usual way, you spoke honestly and to the point. You encouraged me to embrace life.

Julie, an excellent beauty therapist who relaxed me to the point that I had brief moments of nothingness, an empty mind.

Also, thank you brother Steve, for just being Steve.

Nicola and Leanne – fate played a part for Pete and I. This must have been difficult for you to see. Thank you for your understanding and your continued support of all our life plans.

My dear friend Michelle, who listened endlessly whilst giving the facials. You ensured that I looked the best I could, giving me back my confidence. I loved our chats, still do.

Thank you Clacton friends, Carole and Sarah. When contacted, you were here. You were my link between the past and the present.

Mary, you knew how I would be feeling. You offered me guidance and reassurance. I knew that if you could carry a positive attitude then I could. You are a huge inspiration.

The ladies from Rotary, thank you for your chats and support. You listened with interest when I announced that I would one day be the president of the local rotary club! Of course, I had no intention of doing this. Pat and Elffie, thank you.

Huge bear hugs to Jack and Harrison my grandsons. Their love for nannie gave me a purpose, a reason to return to being 'fun nannie'

To my friends who are bereaved, both locally and on the forums. The camaraderie and bond that we have is amazing. Never stop supporting each other.

To the friends that I have finally reconnected with – thank you. You have been sensitive, understanding and above all, patient.

Thank you Orjan for being there at a time when it was needed. You gave me the foresight into seeing that life goes on.

Thank you Ivan, without you, this book would not have been written. Your encouragement and guidance is so very appreciated. The whole experience has been so cathartic, which you said it would be.

I remain so grateful to my nursing colleagues. We work as a team and have the same end goal. We enjoy healthy debate and good banter throughout the shifts. Without even knowing, you have supported my purpose.

AND FINALLY . . .

A pink one! Massive thanks to James and Nura. A baby girl to arrive in April 2022. Soon to be nannie to three!

Useful information

WHEN someone passes away there is so much to do. Hopefully, these next few pages will guide you through what needs to be done and when.

(Sources: Which? Age UK; Gov.UK; Money Advice Service et al)

If death was **unexpected** you should call the family doctor or relative.

If death *was* **expected**, say as a result of a terminal illness, you will need to obtain a medical certificate from the doctor which shows the cause of death. You will then be handed a formal notice which states the doctor has signed the certificate and instructing you how to register the death.

Once the medical certificate has been issued you will be free to instruct a funeral director who will transfer the body to a funeral home.

An **unexpected** death that occurs at home requires the death to be reported to a coroner. A coroner is responsible for investigating an unexpected death. Sometimes a funeral may need to be delayed if the coroner decides to call for a post-mortem or an inquest.

Should the deceased have passed away in hospital, the hospital authorities normally issue a medical certificate and formal notice. Usually the body will remain at the hospital in the mortuary until either the funeral director or relatives arrange for the deceased to be transferred to a chapel of rest or to be taken home.

A death needs to be registered within five days at a register office. This can be done at any office although it is advisable to do so at one in the area where the death occurred. You will need to take with you the medical certificate showing the cause of death and also the deceased's birth certificate, their NHS medical card or number; their marriage or civil partner certificate; their driving licence and proof of their address.

At the office you will need to tell the registrar the person's full name, if applicable their maiden name; their date and place of birth; their date and place of death; their usual address; their most recent occupation; whether or not they were receiving any state benefits, including State Pension; and the name, occupation, and date of birth of their spouse or civil partner.

Once furnished with the above information the registrar should provide you with a certificate for burial or cremation; and a certificate of registration of death which you should complete and return in its pre-paid envelope if the deceased had been in receipt of State Pension or any benefits.

Sometimes it is necessary to obtain extra death certificates. It is recommended to purchase extra copies as soon as possible as to leave this till later could prove much more expensive. These will be required for the will or any claims to pensions or savings etc and photocopies will not be accepted by many banks or insurance companies.

The *Tell Us Once* service can prove very useful in as much as it is possible to report a death and the service will then contact other government departments on your behalf. You can arrange an appointment with the *Tell Us Once* service when registering a death. Alternatively, you can access the service online or over the phone. To do this you will first need to acquire a *Tell Us Once* reference number from the registrar.

There are a wide number of organisations that will need to be notified in the event of a death and it is advisable to get this done sooner rather than later. These will include some, or all

of the following: libraries; electoral services; council tax services; the tax office; the Driver and Vehicle Licensing Agency (DVLA); the UK Passport Agency and the HMRC for tax purposes.
Driving licences should be returned to the DVLA while passports should be returned to HM Passport Office.

Other organisations will need to contacted. These include, where relevant: pension scheme providers; insurance companies; banks and building societies; employers; mortgage providers; housing associations and council housing offices; utility companies; doctors; dentists; opticians; other relevant medical organisations; charities or organisations or magazine subscriptions that have been taken out in the deceased's name and, finally, the Bereavement Register in order to remove the deceased's details from various mailing lists. This should also help prevent the receipt of most advertising mail.

If you are responsible for a Lasting or Enduring Power of Attorney you should notify the Office of the Public Guardian and furnish them with a death certificate.

Before planning a funeral, it is best to check whether or not the deceased had left any instructions for this. Check their will or search for any letter that may outline their wishes. If no such wish list can be found it is normally left to the executor or the nearest relative to decide what type of funeral – burial or cremation – should take place.
It is important that any funeral director chosen is registered. Check on this. Are they members of the National Association of Funeral Directors or the National Society of Allied and Independent Funeral Directors?
Also, bear in mind that prices can vary considerably. To be sure you get value for money make sure you get more than one quote, preferably itemised to include the funeral director's services; a coffin; transfer of the deceased person from the place of death and the care of them prior to the funeral; a

hearse to the nearest crematorium or cemetery and, finally, all necessary arrangements and paperwork.
Bear in mind there could be extra expense in respect of third parties such as the crematorium, clergy and doctors. Funeral directors may ask for these fees to be paid upfront.

Many people do not realise that it is possible to arrange a funeral without the services of a funeral director. It is possible to arrange a 'do-it-yourself' funeral instead. Such a funeral can be far less expensive, sometimes more environmentally friendly, while also being more personal and intimate.
Usually such funerals transpire as the wishes of the deceased, wishes that had been made clear and often planned by the deceased person in advance. If you wish to arrange such a funeral you will need to contact your local council first of all.
There are a number of ways to pay for a funeral which is a good thing as not everyone has a pile of money laying around for such an occasion. That, however, doesn't mean your loved one cannot have a decent send-off. Nevertheless, think carefully about what can be afforded before planning too much.
So, where will the money come from? Well, it could come from family members or friends or, maybe from a lump sum from a life insurance policy or pension scheme that the deceased had paid into.
Alternatively, check whether the deceased had taken out a pre-paid funeral plan or whether the deceased's estate (i.e. money, property or assets) can cover the cost. Bear in mind funeral costs take precedence over other debts.
Even if the deceased had money in a bank or building society, they are not obliged to release the funds until probate has been granted – this being the legal process of distributing the money, property and possessions of the person who has died. Sometimes this causes a delay, in which case you may be required to pay the funeral costs in the meantime.
A Funeral Payment from the Social Fund is a vital service if you are on a low-enough income to meet the criteria, however

there are strict rules in place about who can get help and how much they can receive. Applicants must be claiming Pension Credit or certain other means-tested benefits, and had a close relationship with the person who died – for instance, you may have been their partner.

Finally, if you don't qualify for a Funeral Payment, or it does not cover the full amount of the funeral, it may be advisable to check whether or not you can acquire a Budgeting Loan from the Social Fund. These are interest-free loans of between £100 and £1,500 that you will be required to repay from your benefits.

Useful contacts

Details as applicable at time of writing (2022).

Tell Us Once Bereavement Advice Service:
www.gov.uk/ tellusonce
When you register a death with the registry office the *Tell Us Once* service will provide you with a unique reference number which will enable you to access the *Tell Us Once* service online or by telephone via 0800 085 7308.

The Driver and Vehicle Licensing Agency (DVLA):
www.gov.uk/dvla
If the *Tell Us Once* service is not available in your area you should inform the DVLA that the person has died. You should include that person's driving licence and state your relationship to the deceased; the date they died, their full name, address and date of birth. Send the letter to: DVLA, Swansea, SA99 1AD. You do NOT need to send a death certificate. Telephone 0300 790 6808.

The UK Passport Agency:
General enquiries: HM Passport Office, PO Box 767, Southport, PR8 9PW. Telephone 0300 222 0000. 8am-8pm Mon-Fri; 9am-5.30pm weekends/holidays.

The Public Guardian
(re Lasting or Enduring Power of Attorney):
www.gov.uk/browse/births-deaths-marriages/lasting-power-attorney
Telephone 0300 456 0300
Email customerservices@publicguardian.gsi.gov.uk
Opening hours: Mon, Tues, Thurs, Fri 9.30am-5pm; Weds 10am-5pm.

The HMRC:
www.gov.uk/contact-hmrc or 0300 200 3300.

The Social Fund
(re Funeral Payments or Budgeting Loans):
For Funeral Payments telephone the Bereavement Service on 0800 731 0464 – option 2.
For a Budgeting Loan, you will need first of all to check your eligibility. You cannot receive a Budgeting Loan if you are in receipt of Universal Credit. Instead, you will need to apply for a Budgeting Advance.
To be eligible for a Budgeting Loan, you or your partner must be receiving one of the following benefits: Pension Credit; Income Support; Income-based Jobseeker's Allowance; Income-based Employment and Support Allowance.
You may have different options for repaying your loan but you will need to repay it within 104 weeks. What you owe is usually taken out of your benefit payments until the loan is paid off. Visit www.gov.uk to download a claim form SF500 or contact Jobcentre Plus on 0800 055 6688 to apply for a Budgeting Loan.

Bereavement UK:
www.bereavement.co.uk
email: support@bereavement.co.uk

Age UK Advice:
www.ageuk.org.uk
0800 678 1602 every day from 8am to 7pm.

Turn2Us:
A charitable organisation helping people access the money available to them through welfare benefits, grants and other help.
www.turn2us.org.uk
Telephone 0808 802 2000.

Citizens Advice:
A national network of advice centres offering free, confidential, independent advice, either by telephone or face-to-face. Telephone: 0800 144 8848. Mon-Fri 9am-5pm. Usually busiest at the beginning and end of the day. Not available on public holidays.

-oOo-

Other books by Ivan Sage

The Party's Over . . . Living Without Leah – Robson Books
Leah Betts, the Legacy of Ecstasy – Robson Books
Lawford Life – IRS Publications
Some Mother's Son – Millenium Press
Out of the Shadows – John Blake Books
Not Stupid – John Blake Books
The Gift of Time – a Pat Prestney Publication
Calcraft – Britain's Longest-Serving Hangman (10 volumes)
- Kindle

-oOo-